Eat Your Feelings

Eat Your Feelings

RECIPES FOR SELF-LOATHING

HEATHER WHALEY

HUDSON
STREET
PRESS

HUDSON STREET PRESS
Published by the Penguin Group
Penguin Group (USA) Inc., 375 Hudson Street, New York, New York 10014, U.S.A.
Penguin Group (Canada), 90 Eglinton Avenue East, Suite 700, Toronto, Ontario, Canada M4P 2Y3
(a division of Pearson Penguin Canada Inc.)
Penguin Books Ltd., 80 Strand, London WC2R 0RL, England
Penguin Ireland, 25 St. Stephen's Green, Dublin 2, Ireland (a division of Penguin Books Ltd.)
Penguin Group (Australia), 250 Camberwell Road, Camberwell, Victoria 3124, Australia
(a division of Pearson Australia Group Pty. Ltd.)
Penguin Books India Pvt. Ltd., 11 Community Centre, Panchsheel Park, New Delhi – 110 017, India
Penguin Group (NZ), 67 Apollo Drive, Rosedale, North Shore 0632, New Zealand
(a division of Pearson New Zealand Ltd.)
Penguin Books (South Africa) (Pty.) Ltd., 24 Sturdee Avenue, Rosebank, Johannesburg 2196, South Africa

Penguin Books Ltd., Registered Offices: 80 Strand, London WC2R 0RL, England

First published by Hudson Street Press, a member of Penguin Group (USA) Inc.

First Printing, October 2009
1   3   5   7   9   10   8   6   4   2

REGISTERED TRADEMARK—MARCA REGISTRADA

Library of Congress Cataloging-in-Publication Data

Whaley, Heather.
Eat your feelings : recipes for self-loathing / Heather Whaley.
p.   cm.
ISBN 978-1-59463-059-0 (acid-free paper)
1. Cookery—Humor.   2. Recipes—Humor.   3. Self-esteem in women—Humor.   I. Title.
PN6231.C624W48   2009
818'.607—dc22   2009026044

Printed in the United States of America
Set in Avenir and Monterey BT
Designed by Fine Design

For Frank, Buster, and Tallulah—
all good feelings.

Contents

Contents

Contents

Contents

Contents

Contents

Dear Reader,

What you are holding in your hands is not simply a cookbook. In these pages you're not going to find the same tired old recipes with tedious instructions: add a "dab of this" and a "dash of that." This won't be merely a guide to roasting the perfect pork tenderloin, braising root vegetables fresh from the farmers' market, or decorating your tablescape with fresh figs and absurd branches collected from your garden. On the contrary, dear reader, what you are holding is a book about eating. And not just regular eating but eating when you are on a mission, likely a solo mission, one filled with despair and self-loathing, and, most probably, in the dark.

Surely you already know how to make a lovely romantic dinner of sweetbreads in pear jus for that special someone, a sumptuous eight-course tasting menu for out-of-town guests, or poached lobster with truffles and seared foie gras for lunch when you're feeling peckish. But what about all those other special moments? After all, who among us has not woken up after a night of drunken revelry only to have memories of their hideous behavior come crashing down like a freight train of humiliation? Who has not found oneself fired from a dead-end job, middle-aged and living with one's parents? Who has not looked at their spouse and thought, "If he so much as brushes past me, I will rip his head off and drop-kick it across the kitchen like a soccer ball"? And, I ask you, who has not experienced explosive diarrhea in a public place or at their new boyfriend's house? I know I have.

What is there for you to do in such moments? Sure, you could head for the nearest drive-thru or sit in a dark room muttering to yourself, as usual, or perhaps throw open the nearest window and contemplate the plunge. But wait, there is a better way: You can treat yourself right, with delicious, succulent, home-cooked comfort food.

Dear reader, I'd like you to think of this book not only as a collection of delectable treats, but as a hand to hold in those bleak moments——as your very own support group to remind you that you're not alone. You are not alone. Yes, this is a call to arms for all emotional eaters: Stuff your face with something fantastically cheesy, salty, sugary, and soaked in booze. And cry. Don't forget to cry. And when it's over and your distended abdomen can hold no more? Look in the mirror and say aloud, "[insert your name here], it's not your fault that you [insert fault here: binge drink, overeat, are a sex fanatic, accidentally got pregnant, et cetera]." Say it. Even if it is, technically, your fault.

With dearest sympathy,

Heather Whaley

Eat Your Feelings

HAMBURGER CASSEROLE FOR WHEN NOBODY LOVES YOU AND NEVER WILL

You will need:

- ½ lb. ground beef
- 2 cans condensed tomato soup
- ½ box egg noodles
- DVD of *Kramer vs. Kramer* or *Terms of Endearment*
- 1 onion, chopped
- American cheese slices, orange variety
- Salt and pepper

Go to the video store and rent something sad. *Terms of Endearment* is a good one or *Kramer vs. Kramer.*

Once home, preheat oven to 400°F. Brown beef in a pan. Add onions and sauté until beef is cooked and onions translucent. Boil noodles (duh). After you drain noodles, change into your fanciest outfit, since you are unlikely ever to get an opportunity to wear it in public.

In a large bowl, combine condensed soup and beef-and-onion mix. Add noodles and season with salt and pepper. Pour into a baking dish and top with cheese singles. Bake until cheese is melted and bubbly. Eat. Cry. Eat more while watching *Kramer vs. Kramer.* Cry some more. Eat the rest. Repeat for next fifty to seventy years, depending on age and life expectancy.

RUNK AND DISORDERLY DONUT PUDDING

You will need:

1 box donuts, any variety
2 cups milk
¼ tsp. salt
3 egg yolks
⅓ cup sugar
1 tsp. vanilla

Once released from lockup, stop by donut store. Do not take donuts from the station house, as police tend to be territorial about their pastries. When home, preheat oven to 350°F.

Break donuts into large chunks. Warm milk together with salt in a small pot. Vow, with absolute sincerity, that you will never *ever* drink again. Place donut chunks in baking dish. Check fridge to see if you have any beer. You do. Natch. Have one.

Beat egg yolks, sugar, and vanilla. (Don't bother with the electric mixer: a fork will do.) Drizzle into milk, then pour egg mixture over donuts. Put baking dish in a water bath (a larger dish filled partway with water) and bake for 45 minutes.

While it's cooking, enjoy three or four more beers, as desired. Then prank call the officers who busted you last night; tell them you found Mike Oxlong's wallet. Hang up. Enjoy more beer, as available. Take donut pudding out of oven; eat directly from baking dish. Pass out.

When you wake up, go down to precinct and tell the arresting officers in person what they can do with their warrants.

Repeat.

BABY WON'T STOP CRYING NACHOS SUPREME

You will need:

1 bag corn chips
1 container sour cream
1 Tbs. horseradish
1 jar salsa
½ lb. Monterey jack cheese,
  shredded
½ lb. white cheddar cheese,
  shredded
Chili powder

Put baby down gently, fighting urge to shake it. Preheat oven to 350°F. Using your most soothing voice, talk to baby, explaining that you are making nachos. Spread chips on baking sheet. Tell baby that nachos are a delicious treat that someday she will enjoy, particularly in college—if she makes it to college. Realize baby does not understand you—seems, in fact, to cry louder at the sound of your voice. Wonder if baby will always be ungrateful.

Top chips with shredded cheeses and sprinkle with chili powder. Put in oven. Mix horseradish with sour cream.

When cheese is melted, remove from oven. Pick baby up and begin to pace, rocking and bouncing her in intervals of four to ten minutes or until back gives out. Enjoy nachos with sides of sour cream and salsa. Curse generic condom manufacturer for its substandard product.

CD BLT

You will need:

Ziplock bags
Cleanser with bleach
Alternate cleanser with bleach
Bacon
Ruler
Butter lettuce
Antibacterial soap
White bread
Mayonnaise
Alternate antibacterial soap
Tomato

Begin by blowing hard on all surfaces of kitchen to get rid of any germs that may have recently settled there. Wash hands. Use cleanser No. 1 to clean cleanser No. 2; then use cleanser No. 2 to clean all surfaces in kitchen, including bottoms of chairs and table legs. Place both cleansers in clean ziplock bags. Wash hands, being mindful of under-fingernail germs. Throw soap in garbage.

Remove bacon package from refrigerator and quickly trace brand name logo with finger. Remove skillet from ziplock bag, discarding contaminated bag. Wash hands. Using ruler, place desired number of bacon strips in skillet exactly ¾ of an inch apart, and cook over medium heat. Wash hands. Remove bread from ziplock bag; quickly trace brand name logo with finger. You must do this fast! Faster! If not fast enough, use hand to slap self. Wash hands.

Place two slices of white bread in toaster and set dial to 6. Wash hands. Remove tomato from ziplock bag, discarding contaminated bag. Slice two exactly identical rounds from innermost portion of tomato (you may have to use several tomatoes to achieve identical widths). Discard remainder of tomato(es). Wash hands. Remove lettuce from ziplock bag, discarding contaminated bag. Remove two pieces of exactly identical color from interior portion of lettuce, discarding rest. Use ruler to cut lettuce into perfect ¾-inch squares.

Wash hands.

Remove mayonnaise from refrigerator, take out of ziplock bag, and discard bag. Quickly, using finger—really quickly—trace mayonnaise logo, really fast. Wash hands. Smear mayonnaise on bread; top with bacon, lettuce, and tomato; measure into perfect halves using ruler and cut. Wash hands.

Count to seventy-three as fast as you can. If you stumble on a number, you must begin again. This can take anywhere from thirty seconds to four hours. Enjoy sandwich. Wash hands.

BEST FRIEND IS A TOTAL BITCH GRILLED CHEESE SANDWICH

You will need:

Two slices sourdough bread
Butter, lots of it
Cheese, any variety,
   but Gruyère rules
Bacon

As you stand there wondering why she can't just swear that she didn't sleep with your boyfriend—how hard is that question?—slice cheese (much like you would like to slice her throat). Saying she didn't and acting all indignant is not the same as swearing on her mother's life. And she's such a bitch for *refusing* to swear on her mother's life and for acting like *you* did something wrong by asking her to do it.

In a skillet, melt enough butter to coat pan. Place one slice of bread in skillet and top with cheese, bacon, more cheese, and bread. Push down on sandwich with spatula as you play the conversation out for the fiftieth time:

> **You:** So why is everyone saying that you slept with my boyfriend?
>
> **Former BFF:** I don't know what you're talking about.
>
> **You:** Are you kidding me?
>
> **Former BFF:** No.
>
> **You:** Like, everybody's been saying that you totally hooked up with him.
>
> **Former BFF:** Ew. No. I would never. In the first place, I wouldn't do that to you, and, in the second place, he is *so* not hot.
>
> **You:** Why are you such a bitch?
>
> **Former BFF:** Oh am I? *I'm* a bitch because your boyfriend is a dog and cheats on you?

You: Why can't you just swear on it?

Former BFF: Don't insult me.

You: Just swear. Swear on the life of your mother.

Former BFF: Whatever!

Flip sandwich, adding more butter to the pan. Press down to crisp up bottom. Think for a moment that perhaps she didn't sleep with him. Decide that is impossible—the bitch is a total slut, and she's always been jealous of you. When cheese is melted and both sides browned, turn onto a plate and enjoy. Call boyfriend to see if he wants to hang out later.

THE WHOLE OFFICE READ YOUR JOURNAL YUMMY OATMEAL MUFFINS

You will need:

1 egg
1 cup buttermilk
½ cup brown sugar
½ cup oil
1 cup quick-cooking oats
1 cup flour
1 tsp. baking powder
1 tsp. salt
½ tsp. baking soda
A person with the same
   name as you

Another boring day at the office. Oh! Here comes Laurie from accounting. She's smiling—she must have a good joke. What's this? She hands you a familiar-looking book. "This was in with the fact sheets in the copy room," she says with a grin. You smile back but can hardly conceal your sense of dread. She leaves, and eventually you dare to look at the book in your hands. It is, indeed, the journal you lost over a year ago.

If you can't fake a dentist appointment, put aside all thoughts of your innermost confessions having become fodder for the office gossip mill until the end of the workday.

Once safely home, preheat oven to 400°F. Place muffin cups into a muffin pan. Open journal to see exactly what everyone knows about you. Read:

Dear Diary,

The new boss arrived today. His name is Steven, and he is super sexy. He has really wavy dark hair and strong shoulders. I just know he's going to totally turn the department around. Maybe he'll give me a special project to work on! That would show Laurie from accounting. She always treats me like a complete idiot. She's such a bitch.

In a medium-size bowl, beat egg and stir in milk, sugar, and oil. Beat again to combine. Read:

Eat Your Feelings

Dear Diary,

I had such horrible diarrhea all day long and had to keep running to the toilet. I'm not really sure how it happened, but I got some poop on the floor of the bathroom——I think because I literally had to run in there 'cause I was about to explode, and when I whipped down my pants, I think I was already going. I thought I made it in time, but I guess some leaked onto the floor. Anyway, when I stood up, sure enough, I slipped and landed on my rear, in the poo, on the floor, like a fish outta water. It got all over my pants. I tried to scrub it out and ended up sopping wet, with a huge stain. I had to quickly run out of the office to get something else to wear. Thank God there is Gap across the street. And thank God they had a bathroom.

Stir in remaining ingredients until moist. Keep reading:

Dear Diary,

Today I think I made progress with Steven! I have been sort of hanging around his office as much as I can. I can't help it, really. He's all I think about. At night, when I'm home, I look at his photo on the company Web site. Sometimes I set up my computer across from me as I eat my Lean Cuisine dinner and pretend we're dining together in a fancy restaurant. We have the greatest talks this way. Anyway, I practiced telling him something *funny. It was something my mom had told me, a joke about a woman who is too busy to remember she has kids. And I went into his office and said, really casual, "Oh, hey there, Steven. Did you hear the one about the woman who was so busy she didn't remember she had kids?" He gave me* <u>*THE MOST GENUINE*</u> *smile. I don't care if everyone says he is gay.*

As you picture your coworkers and Steven (oh God, Steven!) huddled together in the copy room, laughing their heads off, pour batter into the muffin cups till they are about ⅔ full. Bake for 20 minutes or until brown. Try to locate someone who shares your name, so you can claim the diary is not yours. Of course, this person must also work in your office. Eat while warm, perhaps with butter. Feel your heart crumble to dust and disappear.

WORST DATE EVER NUTTY CHEESE BALL

You will need:

2 8 oz. packages cream cheese
1 6½ oz. can crushed pineapple, drained
1½ cups walnuts
¼ cup finely chopped green pepper
1 Tbs. chopped celery

You should have known that it wasn't going to go well when he arrived to pick you up for dinner on his Segway. As if it wasn't awkward enough having to walk briskly along beside him, craning your neck to make eye contact as he rolled down the sidewalk, there was the added talking point of his jaunty little straw boater. What was he thinking? What were you?

Now you are starving because he took you to a raw food restaurant and then announced that everything was, "Real expensive, so don't go crazy." You were totally not prepared for him to whip out the calculator to determine, to the penny, what you ate. Once safely back in your own apartment—alone!—make yourself a nutty cheese ball because that's exactly what that clown was. Mix together cream cheese and pineapple.

Take a quick peek out the window to make sure he's gone. What? Is that him, lurking beneath the lamppost? Oh great, not only was he a lousy date, but now he wants to *stalk* you? Why is it always the losers that you can't get rid of? Wonder, "Why can't the really good-looking and successful guys be the stalkers?" as you put walnuts in a ziplock bag and crush them with a hammer, pounding on them like he kept pounding his fist on the table as he ranted endlessly about how nobody listens to him at work.

Add diced green pepper and celery to the cheese. Roll cheese mixture into a ball. Try not to think about how he kept adjusting his balls during dinner, saying, "Damn, boys, sit still!" And especially don't think about the several times he actually reached down inside his pants and then with the same hand reached over to your plate to fish a piece of zucchini out of your raw lasagna.

Roll cheese ball in walnuts and vow not to ever, ever again go out with a man you met at the ninety-nine-cent store.

YOUR BROTHER REALLY WAS MOM'S FAVORITE PEACH PIE

You will need:

⅔ cup packed golden brown sugar
¼ cup flour
1 tsp. fresh lemon juice
½ tsp. ground cinnamon
¼ tsp. ground ginger
3 lb. peaches, nectarines, or a
   combination of both
2 frozen piecrusts, defrosted

Eat Your Feelings

Preheat oven to 375°F. Call your mom to get recipe for peach pie. When she dismisses you, as usual, saying that she's "really busy right now," call brother. Hang up when he says, "I'm talking to Mom. What do you want?" Go to cupboard for great-grandmother's Wedgwood pie dish that has been handed down through the family. Remember at last minute that brother has it. Poke holes in one piecrust, line with aluminum foil, fill with beans or pie weights, and prebake piecrust in oven until barely golden brown.

Realize pie recipe uses metric system, which utterly confounds you. Maybe it wouldn't if you'd been sent to a fancy private school or an elite college like your brother. Unfortunately, your mother spent your college fund on your brother's graduation present, a round-the-world trip for the two of them.

Peal peaches and cut into eighths. Toss in a bowl with remaining ingredients and let stand for 30 minutes to 1 hour, or just long enough to dig out that old manuscript your mom wrote about the mother with two children who are kidnapped. In the story, the mother finds the older brother, who in turn helps bust the kidnapper, but when she locates the younger daughter, living with a new family in Arizona, she realizes that kid is better off where she is and leaves her there. Weep great, heaving sobs, being mindful not to forget about peaches.

Spoon filling into prebaked crust. Lay second crust on top and seal edge in a decorative fashion, making several slits in dough to vent. Bake until golden and bubbling, about 1 hour and 20 minutes. Enjoy à la mode or with dollop of resentment.

FAILED THE GED CREAMED SPINACH FOR IDIOTS

You will need:

Adult supervision
1 Tbs. olive oil (liquid, not cartoon character)
1 bunch spinach (a vegetable)
1 clove garlic, minced (*minced* means "chopped into teeny-weeny pieces")
2 Tbs. butter
1 Tbs. flour
½ cup cream
¼ cup bread crumbs
2 Tbs. Parmesan cheese (this is the kind of cheese you put on spaghetti)
Salt and pepper

Preheat oven to 325°F. In other words, turn the oven to "Bake," set the temperature knob (the one with the numbers) to 325, and wait until it either beeps or a light goes on or off, depending on the oven's age and model.

In a large saucepan, heat olive oil over medium-high heat. Add spinach and garlic; sauté until wilted (*sauté* means "to stir is around until it's all cooked"). Drain spinach in a colander (one of those bowls with all the holes in the bottom). In the same pan, heat butter over medium heat and when melted add flour, stirring nonstop for 2 minutes. Add cream and continue stirring. Put spinach back into pan and swoosh around until coated with cream.

In a bowl, mix cheese and bread crumbs together. It is better to do this with a spoon than with your fingers.

Get a baking dish and smear the inside with butter. Pour spinach in bowl and cover with cheese and bread crumbs. Bake in oven for 10 minutes or until top is golden brown. Turn oven off so as not to burn down house. Consider a career in one of the following: professional athletics, motion pictures, politics, or lawn care.

**Y**OU WALKED ALL THE
WAY TO YOUR OFFICE WITHOUT
REALIZING YOUR SKIRT WAS
TUCKED INTO YOUR UNDERPANTS
SESAME CHICKEN

You will need:

Pants

It is a glorious morning! The sun is shining, there isn't a cloud in the sky, and you are feeling great in your flirty new skirt as you saunter down the sidewalk to the train. Hel-*lo*! Who is that cutie giving you the eye? You look back, and he's still checking you out. A third look confirms that he's following you. He's far too cute to be a weirdo; it must be your lucky day! You begin to notice that every Tom, Dick, and Harry you come across seems to be checking you out. Must have been something in your oatmeal!

You hop on the train, smiling coyly to yourself and to the gorgeous men who are totally distracted and disarmed by you. At your stop, you prance out the door and up the stairs, fully aware that you have suddenly become the pied piper of men of all kinds. There's the hottie from before, as well as a few notties and a slew of other fine fellows following you up the stairs.

Wait, why is this little old lady grabbing you? What could *she* possibly want? "Wha . . . ? My skirt is . . . what? Oh . . . Thanks . . ."

Jump into a taxi and head home. Once there, lock the door, shut all the blinds, pick up the phone, and order an extra-large sesame chicken from the closest Chinese restaurant.

For the next few days, check YouTube to be sure your indecent exposure wasn't captured on film. Phew. Then check XTube . . . Damn.

Wear pants.

YOUR DECOR HASN'T CHANGED SINCE COLLEGE PIZZA LOAF

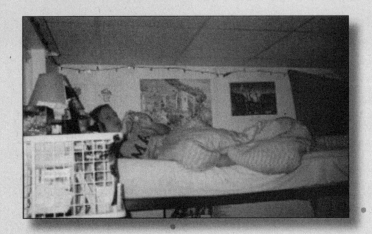

You will need:

2 lb. ground beef
½ lb. sweet Italian sausage
1 cup saltines
2 cloves garlic, minced
1 onion, chopped
1 egg
1 15 oz. can tomato sauce
2 tsp. salt
¾ tsp. oregano
½ tsp. pepper
3 oz. grated mozzarella cheese
5 green olives, sliced

Eat Your Feelings

In milk crate next to futon, find box of saltines and crush crackers until you have 1 cup or enough to fill the bottom chamber of your skeleton bong. In a hot pot, mix spices with tomato sauce, reserving ½ tsp. oregano. Take sausage out of casing and crumble. If the sausage seems to be moving, don't worry: it's just the glow from the lava lamp. Mix sausage with beef, cracker crumbs, garlic, onion, and egg.

Preheat toaster oven to 350°F. It may be necessary to unplug Christmas lights lining ceiling to do so. Add 10 oz. tomato sauce to meat, mixing well and place in a 9 × 5 loaf pan. If you do not have a loaf pan, do not substitute the shoe box where you keep your mix tapes. Instead just form into a loaflike shape in whatever pan you have available. Spread remaining tomato sauce on top of loaf and bake for 1 hour and 30 minutes. During this time you may stare at your 3-D unicorn art, relax in your butterfly chair listening to Pink Floyd, practice your Hacky Sack skills, rearrange posters, or think about growing up a little.

Sprinkle top of loaf with grated cheese and oregano, and top with olive slices. Bake for 5–10 minutes or until cheese is melted. Let stand for 10 minutes and then serve. If no plates are available, use spare Frisbees.

KY-HIGH BANANA CREAM PIE
BECAUSE YOU ARE DATING A
MARRIED GUY

You will need:

1 frozen piecrust
4 bananas
2 boxes vanilla pudding
4 cups milk
4 cups cream
½ cup sugar

Eat Your Feelings

Preheat oven to 350°F. Poke holes in piecrust and bake for 10 minutes or until golden brown. Slice bananas. Check voice mail to see if he's called you. He hasn't. Prepare pudding according to package directions. Check voice mail again.

Place bananas in crust and cover with pudding. Pick up telephone to make sure the line isn't dead. It isn't.

In a large bowl, mix the cream and sugar. Whip with an electric mixer until thick and whippy. Call his house. When the wife answers, hang up quickly! Do not succumb to urge to tell her about the torrid but empty affair you are having with her husband. As tempting as it is, think of what it would do to the children. Top pie with whipped cream.

Go into bathroom, or to nearest mirror, and stare at your wretched self while repeating, "Idiot. Idiot. Idiot. Idiot." Bring pie into bathroom and eat while staring at yourself in the mirror, so you can see just how disgusting you truly are.

ALAPEÑO POPPERS FOR WHEN YOUR ONLY FRIENDS ARE PEOPLE YOU MET IN A CHAT ROOM

You will need:

12 oz. cream cheese, softened
1 8 oz. pack shredded
  Mexican-blend cheeses
1 Tbs. crumbled bacon
Sunlight and fresh air
12 oz. can jalapeños, drained
  and cut in half
1 cup milk
1 cup flour
1 cup bread crumbs
Oil for frying

Mix together cheeses and bacon and stuff into jalapeños. Resist urge to check Facebook to see if anyone has poked *you* in last 10 minutes. They haven't, as they have real friends. Look out the window. See those people? They are real, not avatars. Wonder what their avatars look like.

Place milk into one bowl, flour in another, and play your move on Lexulous. Laugh at Jen4Evah's playing of the word "boobies." Jen4Evah is awesome. Dunk peppers first into milk, then into flour. Place bread crumbs in a third bowl. Dunk peppers again in milk and then in bread crumbs. Repeat to make peppers extra crispy.

Film quick video protesting Twitter's new disclosure policy, being sure to talk in superlatives and a crazy-sounding accent to ensure maximum hits when you upload it to iReport. Fry peppers in oil until golden brown, about 3 minutes each. Enjoy with your favorite beverage, taking care not to drip cheese onto keyboard as drips and spills are not covered by AppleCare.

$\mathcal{F}$ORECLOSURE FIESTA

You will need:

Spare change
6 avocados
1 lime
1 clove garlic, halved
1 small onion, chopped
Small bunch cilantro, chopped
1 tomato, chopped
Salt

Arrange four chairs—you know, the ones that have yet to be repossessed—in a semicircle for the few friends who haven't abandoned you. Take jar of change to nearest Coinstar machine; use proceeds ($56.34) to buy ingredients and rent frozen-margarita machine. (Note: in parts of the western United States, limes and avocados grow on trees and may be procured by shimmying up trunk and self-picking.)

Use extra-long extension cord to siphon electricity from neighbor for margarita machine. Soak onion in juice of one lime. Mash avocado into a bowl that has been rubbed with garlic. Add onions and all other ingredients and season with salt.

Should repo man arrive for chairs, invite him in and serve guacamole with chips. The more the merrier! When party is over, do not feel despondent; look on the bright side: no more annoying mortgage payments or nosy neighbors to worry about *and* there is no need to clean up. Simply pack leftovers in a cooler and go sit in the park.

WHO'S THE DADDY? FLAPJACKS

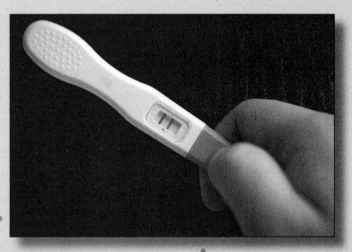

You will need:

- 1½ cups flour
- 3 Tbs. melted butter, plus some for frying
- 3 Tbs. sugar
- 2 eggs
- 1¼ cups milk
- 1 tsp. salt
- 1¾ tsp. baking soda
- ¼ tsp. cinnamon
- ¼ tsp. vanilla
- ¼ tsp. saliva from each possible daddy
- DNA testing kit

Eat Your Feelings

While looking at your baby's face, subtract all similarities to yourself and see which of the many possible fathers the baby resembles. When this proves ineffective—as it no doubt will, given the very many men you slept with nine and a half months ago—mix flour, sugar, salt, and baking soda in a bowl. Remember with annoyance how the nurses reacted to your surprise that the baby didn't have darker skin. Phone Kyle, Brad, Philemon, Bo Jing, and George to explain that you need to get some saliva from them. You might not want to tell them straight off why you want it. Maybe say that you want to wear it in a vial around your neck.

Beat together eggs, milk, and melted butter. Add cinnamon and vanilla. Suddenly recall Zander, Tito, Aafiya, and the Dude. Call the first three, and send the Dude a text message. He never picks up the phone. Oh! Don't forget N!xau. Write *him* a letter.

Combine egg mix with flour and stir well. Heat butter in a pan and pour in ½ cup batter. Cook until done on one side and flip to cook the other side. Enjoy with sugar, syrup, or birth control pills.

FORTY YEARS OLD AND FIRED FROM STARBUCKS CHEWY FRUIT AND NUT COOKIE STACK

You will need:

Large pockets

Eat Your Feelings

After Laurie is finished reading the lengthy list of your infractions (not knowing the difference between an Americano and a macchiato, a distaste for Bob Dylan, waving your hand in front of your nose and saying PU when someone orders soy milk), head home with your pockets full of goodies to tide you over until you find another job.

Open one pack madeleines, being careful not to strain your carpal-tunnel-affected wrist (curse that incessant foaming). Place one madeleine on plate.

Make a list of pros and cons of being fired from the Bucks.

Pros:

No longer have to work for self-important seventeen-year-old Laurie

No more apron

Don't have to listen to overcaffeinated eighty-year-old ladies talk about gout

No more having to go to the bathroom every ten minutes

Dan Zanes–free afternoons

Can sleep late

Can watch television all day

Are too old to work at Starbucks in any case

Cons:

Have to pay for coffee

Not getting paid

Have to get another job

Are totally unqualified to do anything but work at Starbucks

Take one Chewy Fruit and Nut bar, layer it between two madeleines. Top with one Fruit Stella™ from pocket. Call mother and ask if you can stay at her house for a while—tell her you will bring a pound of Café Estima Blend© Fair Trade Certified™ ground for her Mr. Coffee machine. Take one-pound bag of said coffee out of pants, where it has been chafing since you shoved it down there on your way out the door.

Place remaining madeleine on top of Fruit Stella™ and smush down with the palm of your hand, the way your ego was squashed when Laurie chewed you out in front of all the regulars this morning for filling your mouth with whipped cream directly from the can. Who *doesn't* do that? Remember how humiliating it was when everyone was staring at you, and the whipped cream was falling in globs onto your apron. Sandwich the stack between two black-and-white cookies. Shove as much of the Chewy Fruit and Nut cookie stack as you can into your mouth at once. Walk to Jamba Juice; fill out application.

 ## RAVY CHEESE FRIES FOR A BIG FAT FATTY

You will need:

1 bag frozen french fries
1 can chicken gravy
1 packet shredded cheddar cheese
Potato chips
Mayonnaise

Remove constricting Spanx that have been holding in your excess flab like a sausage casing for the past nine hours. Preheat oven to 350°F. Spread fries on baking sheet. Bake according to package directions. Remove from oven, top with cheese, and return to oven for 5 minutes, or until cheese melts. Meanwhile, open can of gravy and heat. Any cheese not used in fry topping can be eaten in reckless fistfuls while you wait for fries to cook. (But, of course, you already know that.)

When cheese is melted, remove from oven, dump into a large bowl (or trough) and top with gravy. Retrieve potato chips from between sofa cushions and sprinkle on top for added crunch. Serve with side of mayonnaise for dipping.

NOBODY THINKS YOU ARE FUNNY ORANGE-GLAZED PORK CHOPS

You will need:

1 Tbs. butter
1 clove garlic
Half onion, minced
1 tsp. ground cumin
Better material
1 cup orange juice
2 pork chops
2 Tbs. olive oil
Timing
Salt and pepper

Melt butter in a medium pan over moderate heat. Add onion, garlic, and cumin and sauté until soft, about 7 minutes. Add orange juice and simmer for 15 minutes.

Meanwhile, salt and pepper pork chops and sauté over medium-high heat until fully cooked. As tempting as it is to eat them raw so as to inflict death upon yourself from salmonella, don't. There are plenty of people that may one day find your personality tolerable. It should come as a relief that you have finally realized after thirty-four years that your go-to joke (A sandwich walks into a bar, and the bartender says, "We don't serve food in here") is just not funny. Neither are jokes about insurance premiums, tax codes, and incurable diseases that afflict children. Nor is a joke made funnier by prefacing it with "Did you ever notice," by saying "That was a joke," or after drinking half a bottle of tequila. And if you have to ask, "Get it?" They didn't.

When chops are fully cooked, pour sauce over them, scraping up little brown bits on bottom of pan. Turn onto plate and enjoy as best you can.

OCKTAIL NIBBLES FOR ALCOHOLICS

You will need:

1 package Pillsbury Grands
  Frozen Biscuits
Small wedge of brie, cut
  into chunks
Dried cranberries
1 cup chopped walnuts,
  if desired

Step 1

Wake to find that you are sleeping next to complete stranger. Quietly get up, and examine said stranger's apartment for indication of who he is and what city you are in. The phone book is a good start. Scranton? Oh boy. Not again. Quietly phone taxi company.

Step 2

Once home, take two Tylenol and one Aleve and hope for the best. Sleep for seven to ten hours, drooling as desired.

Step 3

When you wake, pour ¾ cup alcohol into a glass and drink. Vodka works. If no vodka is available, the following may be substituted: whiskey, rum, gin, schnapps, Listerine.

Step 4

Open package Pillsbury Grands. Preheat oven to 350°F. Separate biscuits and place one into each well of muffin tin. Pour 1 cup vodka into glass. Drink.

Step 5

Place one or two chunks of brie on top of each biscuit. Listen to messages; delete disappointed, judgmental one from passive-aggressive AA sponsor.

Step 6

Call friend and nonchalantly invite her over for some cocktails. If you are drinking Listerine, this is a good opportunity to ask her to bring vodka.

Be sure to do it subtly. Try, "If you happen to be passing by a liquor store . . ."

Step 7

Place a few dried cranberries and walnuts, if using, on top of cheese and pop into oven. Take shower to remove clammy film left by excessive sweating.

Step 8

Check oven. When nibbles are golden brown and puffy, much like your face, remove from oven and cool on a wire rack.

Step 9

Cut each biscuit into four bites, arrange decoratively on a serving dish to accompany vodka when it arrives with enabler.

Step 10

Enjoy cheese nibbles with vodka, taking care to occasionally acknowledge presence of enabler.

Step 11

When vodka is gone, suggest to enabler that you pop out to local bar. Once at bar, forget all about enabler and pay close attention to the kind gentleman who is buying your drinks. Try to get a good look at his face, however blurry it may be. If you have a camera on your cell phone, you may want to take a picture. It could come in handy later.

Step 12

Agree that you and your new gentleman friend should continue your conversation back at his place. So what if it's in Scranton?

POST-TRAUMATIC STRESS DISORDER SWEET POTATO PIE

You will need:

2 medium sweet potatoes
½ stick butter
1 buddy
¾ cup sugar
¾ cup whole milk
3 eggs
1 tsp. vanilla
½ tsp. cinnamon
¼ tsp. salt
1 Tbs. flour
1 piecrust

First, stop shouting. Preheat oven to 350°F. Prick sweet potatoes with a fork and roast them until tender, about 1¼ hours. Seriously, dude, calm down.

Increase oven temperature to 400°F and place a baking pan on the bottom rack. Scoop potatoes from skins and mash with a fork. No, nobody is trying to break into your foxhole. Chill *out!* Melt butter in a small pan, stir in sugar then add to sweet potatoes. Crack eggs as you would skulls and whisk into potato mixture. Whisk in remaining ingredients.

Phone buddy, as you need a voice of reason to tell you that nobody is trying to get you. You are home, making sweet potato pie. *Relax.* Pour filling into piecrust.

Place the piecrust on heated baking dish in oven and bake until set, about 40 minutes. Whoa! Where'd you go? Hello? Why are you staring off into space like that? It's creepy. Snap out of it.

TINKING NO GOOD BROKEDOWN CAR BUTTERMILK FRIED CHICKEN

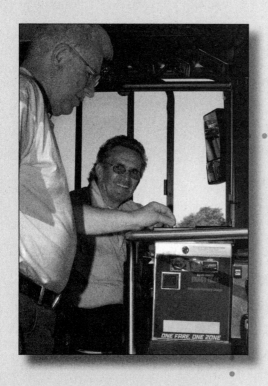

You will need:

Bus pass
4 chicken breasts, bone
  in, skin on
2 cups buttermilk
1 Tbs. salt
1 Tbs. paprika
½ tsp. cayenne
Flour
Oil for frying
Alarm clock

Set alarm clock for two hours earlier than you would have to get up if your car weren't a piece of junk. Put chicken breasts in a plastic bag filled with buttermilk and place in the refrigerator. Once in driveway, pause at vehicle to kick it thirteen times or until your aggression has been sufficiently satisfied. Walk mile and a half to bus stop. Be sure to dress appropriately for the weather, as you will have to wait twenty-seven minutes for the bus.

Take bus seven miles, or one hour and twenty minutes, to workplace. After work, repeat, taking bus for one hour and twenty minutes. From your stop, walk mile and a half to your home while cursing the Russians for producing second-rate vehicles, and yourself for buying one off craigslist.

Pour oil into a heavy skillet or cast-iron pan. The oil should reach halfway up the sides of the pan. Heat to 325°F. Drain chicken of excess buttermilk. If friends should call, entice them with a fried-chicken-themed slumber party, in the hopes that they might stay the night, thereby ensuring you a ride to work in the morning. Rub chicken all over with spice mixture and dredge in flour.

Try to donate vehicle to a charitable organization that will remove it from your property.

Fry chicken in oil until golden brown, about 5 minutes on each side. Drain on a wire rack and plan what to do with the car, as it will surely sit on your lawn for the next fifteen years or until you can afford to have it towed. Some possibilities are: Decide it's a sculpture and charge admission to your gallery, plant a garden inside the hood like the neighbors have done, claim it used to belong to Bruce Willis and sell it on eBay.

PICY NUTS WITH HONEY 'CAUSE YOU MARRIED FOR MONEY

You will need:

Cooking spray
1 tsp. salt
¼ tsp. curry powder
¼ tsp. cayenne
¼ tsp. salt
2 cups pecans
2 Tbs. honey
Loud horn

Coat a large nonstick skillet with cooking spray and place over medium-high heat. Mix together cayenne and curry powder. When husband returns from water aerobics class, change his colostomy bag.

Place nuts and honey in pan and sprinkle on salt and spices. If you like, add more cayenne, depending on the constitution of your husband. Stir to coat nuts (the ones on the pan, not his) and cook for 4 minutes or until toasted. While husband is upstairs changing into his afternoon robe, hide in coat closet. When you hear him coming down the electric chair-lift, wait till he is at the bottom and pop out, blasting the loud horn in his face. If this does not stop his heart, put on as much jewelry as you have, reminding yourself that no one lives forever. Enjoy nuts with a large cocktail as you play canasta till four, when it's time to whiz up his dinner in the blender.

HALLOWEEN COSTUME PROVED OFFENSIVE TO ALL YOUR COWORKERS CHOCOLATE SMORGASBORD

You will need:

1 bag trick-or-treat candy
Sensitivity training

First remove wrapper from 1 Reese's Peanut Butter Cup. Eat. Peek out of windows to see if anybody has spray-painted anything on the side of your house. Unwrap 1 mini Baby Ruth bar. Eat.

Draft letter of apology to National Organization for Women. Find 1 Mr. Goodbar. Unwrap and eat.

Draft letter of apology to American Association of People with Disabilities. Locate 1 pack Rolos. Eat.

Draft one letter of apology to Indigenous Peoples Task Force. Eat 1 Peppermint Pattie.

Draft yet another letter of apology to the Hebrew Immigrant Aid Society. Eat 1 Mounds bar and 1 Almond Joy.

Copy last letter, but this time delete Hebrew Immigrant Aid Society and insert NAACP. Cram 1 fistful of candy corn into mouth and eat. Delete NAACP and insert Christian Solidarity International; do the same with African Ancestral Lesbians United for Social Change, Scottish Human Rights Council, Committee of Concerned Scientists, and Forest Peoples Programme.

Take all Tootsie Rolls, unwrap, form into large ball, and eat as if an apple. Make appointment with sensitivity-training officer and take comfort in knowing that nowadays, if you spend a month in rehab, people will forgive you for almost anything.

CHEESE FONDUE BECAUSE YOUR THERAPIST FELL ASLEEP ON YOU

You will need:

6 cups Gruyère, grated
¼ cup flour
1 clove garlic, halved
1 bottle dry white wine
2 Tbs. sherry
Dash pepper
Dash nutmeg
Day-old bread, cubed

Toss cheese with flour and set aside in much the same way your *very serious problems* were so casually set aside by Dr. Sleepyhead. Rub bottom and sides of a pot with garlic. Heat 2½ cups of wine over low heat until small bubbles rise to surface. Feel your own childhood traumas rising to the surface also: like the time third-grade teacher Mrs. Hiesler exposed your naked behind and spanked you in front of the whole class and the time you walked in on your mom and dad—she inexplicably standing on the bed in her bra and underpants and he in his boxers, kneeling at her feet (?). Get tissues so tears do not fall into pot.

Just before wine boils, work cheese in slowly, watching as it dissolves and disappears into the wine just like you disappear into the wine every night in a vain attempt to hide from yourself. Stir constantly, until the fondue bubbles gently. Stir in sherry, pepper, and nutmeg, and pour into fondue pot. Stand directly over pot to better reach cheese and dunk bread into fondue. Drink remaining wine and stop your whining.

V ALENTINE'S DAY PARTY RYES FOR DIVORCÉES

You will need:

1 package hot dogs
½ pound Swiss cheese
1 loaf rye bread
4 gay men
Vodka
Grand Marnier
Cranberry juice
Juice of one lime
Martina McBride CD

Round up all the gals in the subdivision, 'cause this Valentine's Day is going to be a blast! No more sitting at home moping and drooling over Keith Olbermann. Not *this* year. No, ma'am! In a large glass pitcher mix 2 cups vodka, ½ cup Grand Marnier, ½ cup cranberry juice, and lime juice, 'cause you sassy ladies are gonna drink cosmos! Wooo!

Call the boys too—they will *love* this! (Note: If you live in a so-called red state and can't locate 4 gay men, look for attractive, single, good-smelling men over the age of forty.)

Preheat oven to 375°F. Cut hot dogs into small rounds. Place slices of rye bread on a baking sheet, top with hot-dog rounds, and cover with Swiss cheese. Bake in oven until cheese is melted and bread is toasted. Remove from oven, cut each piece of bread into quarters, and arrange on a platter in an attractive fashion.

Eat Your Feelings

When guests arrive, serve cosmos with party ryes. Some suggestions for activities include:

Dance contest to empowering Martina McBride music, using aerobics moves you learned at Curves

Pin the tail on the trophy wife

Watch *First Wives Club* and drink every time Bette Midler delivers snappy insult to ex-husband

Alter old wedding dresses into cute halter tops or jaunty berets

Duck duck Grey Goose

Uh-oh! Sexy Officer Thunder has arrived to issue a noise complaint!*

Most of all, keep the cosmos flowing to ensure a good time for all!

If Officer Thunder has indeed knocked on your door, you may need to see the following recipe.

DMONISHED BY MALE STRIPPER FOR INAPPROPRIATE BEHAVIOR TARRAGON SCRAMBLED EGGS

You will need:

1 Tbs. butter
3 eggs
Swiss cheese
½ Tbs. fresh tarragon, or
   ½ tsp. dried
2 Tbs. diced fresh tomatoes
$200

In a medium nonstick skillet, melt butter over low heat to coat pan. In a small bowl, mix eggs with tarragon and pour into pan. Continue to cook over low heat. Phone attorney and tell him whole awful, embarrassing story, making sure to point out that it was Doris from next door who started it all by taking off *her* clothes, and that never having hired a stripper before, you were ignorant of the rules.

Tell him that Steven (a.k.a. Thunder) is demanding $200 to not tell your ex-husband and screw up your pending alimony settlement. Ask attorney to drop the bribe money at the designated donut shop or back alley (it would be far too humiliating to see Steven again; not that you would recognize him without his badge). When eggs begin to set, add Swiss cheese and scramble by stirring constantly. Season with salt and pepper, and turn onto plate when eggs are just cooked. Top with diced tomatoes as plump as Thunder's stubbly backside.

DOUBLE CRUST APPLE PIE FOR RECREATIONAL BULIMICS

You will need:

Mouthwash
6 Tbs. (¾ stick) unsalted
   butter
2½ lb. firm tart apples, peeled,
   cored, and sliced into ¼-inch
   wedges
½ cup sugar plus 1 Tbs.
   for sprinkling
Tooth-bleaching gel
¼ cup raisins
½ tsp. ground cinnamon
¼ tsp. ground cloves
2 Tbs. freshly squeezed
   lemon juice
2 Tbs. cornstarch
2 frozen piecrusts
1 egg beaten with 2 Tbs.
milk

Melt 3 Tbs. butter in a large, heavy-bottomed sauté pan over medium heat. Add apple wedges and sauté for 3–4 minutes until slightly softened but still holding their shape . . . Actually, you're just going to throw it up anyway. Forget it.

THE SLAMMIN' CHICK FROM THE CLUB WAS NOT AT ALL A CHICK CHICKEN CLUB

You will need:

2 boneless, skinless chicken breasts
White bread
Mayonnaise
Lettuce
Tomato
2 slices bacon
Listerine

Dude, that was so wrong! Rub breasts with oil the same way you rubbed that guy's breasts. No! Don't think about it! Season with salt and pepper and throw chicken on grill.

Toast bread and slice tomato. Remember thinking at the time how curious it was that her face felt a little rough as you were making out. Dunk head in sink full of ice water. Cut off two slices of lettuce, resisting urge to take knife to your wrist. Man, this is so wrong! Call wingman to ask him, "What the fuck, dude?"

When chicken is done, spread mayo on bread, trying not to think of— No! Buddy, this is not something you're going to just *get over*. Especially seeing as how you were trying so hard to get over on that she-male, bro. Place chicken, bacon, lettuce, and tomato on bread. Eat sandwich, wondering what it means that you liked it more than she did.

YOU FARTED LOUDLY IN THE ELEVATOR GREEN CURRY CHICKEN

You will need:

1 tsp. green curry paste
1 14 oz. can coconut milk
½ cup chicken broth
Small can bamboo shoots
Handful fresh basil leaves,
    cut into slivers
2 cups cooked chicken
4 Thai eggplants, cut
    into quarters
Salt
Beano

Combine curry paste and coconut milk. Bring to a boil like the boiling you felt in your lower colon after eating three Jamaican beef patties in the employee cafeteria. Stir for a while, but don't let it burn like the noxious gas that seeped from your innards.

Add stock and return to a boil, trying not to imagine the conversation in the elevator after you got off—when the stench was at its peak. Add bamboo and eggplant, and simmer until eggplant is as tender as the area on your sphincter burned by the passing of the pungent pre-effluvia.

Make a promise to yourself never to eat the ethnic special at lunchtime. Enjoy the irony that you are, at this very moment, making curry. Check your e-mail to see if people are still sending funny notes about your flatulent indiscretion. Couldn't Seth from marketing come up with something better to call you than Señor Fart?

Add chicken and basil, cook for 5 minutes longer, and enjoy with rice and double dose of Beano.

BREAKFAST SANDWICH FOR MORNING-AFTER REGRET

You will need:

Butter
2 eggs
2 slices American cheese
2 slices whole-wheat toast
Mayonnaise
Avocado
Tomato
Tater Tots
Ketchup
2 slices bacon
Coca-Cola

Eat Your Feelings

While ignoring the flashing light on your answering machine—probably angry calls from former friends you've offended—crack eggs into a hot buttered skillet. It's much easier to scramble the eggs but tastier if you don't. When eggs begin to harden, flip them over and top each with a slice of American cheese. Remember with horror that you called Toby's mother a racist and then pointed your finger at her chanting, "Ra-cist! Ra-cist! Ra-cist!" Toast bread.

Pour yourself a Coke. It has to be a real Coke, not a diet Coke, or the nausea-fighting properties will be negated. Have a few sips while you slice some tomato and avocado. Wonder whatever possessed you to tell Sara that she was "packing on the pounds." Sara's never done anything to you.

Preheat oven and cook Tater Tots according to package directions. Catch a glimpse of the massive hickey on your neck and try very hard to remember. Think. You were with your college roommate's husband, hanging out in the stairwell, but who else was there? Oh God! His friend—his little-person friend! Check the lower part of your body for additional hickeys.

While Tater Tots are cooking, place bacon strips on a cookie sheet, put in the oven, and think, "Why? Why? Why did I go to that stupid party?" Pound fist on counter, as desired. Then wonder, "Do little people eat Tater Tots because full-sized potatoes are too big?"

As a general rule, people don't like gossip about their *own* boyfriends. Wish that you had thought of this *before* you told Barbara you know for a *fact* that her fiancé, Stuart, "experimented" with being gay in college, that his breath stinks, and that you're not sure the two are unrelated.

When bread is toasted, smear mayo on each piece and top with tomato, avocado, bacon, and egg.

Eat with Tater Tots dunked in as much ketchup as you can stand. Google "affordable pleasant places to live," because this time an apology or quick stint in rehab isn't going to work.

TOTALLY BOWLEGGED DOUBLE DEVILED EGG(ED) SALAD

You will need:

4 eggs
2 Tbs. mayonnaise
2 tsp. mustard
½ tsp. relish
Paprika
4 slices bread

Like a little penguin, waddle over to stove and plop eggs into a pot of cold water. Be careful not to trip over feet while doing so. Bring water to a boil, cover, and let rest 15 minutes. In front of mirror, practice dancing to see if you really *do* look like you're a Kabuki actor. Yep.

Ride 'em, cowboy, to the fridge and get mayo and mustard. If you have a "galley" kitchen, you will have to turn sideways to get in there, as your knees splay out to the side too much for regular straight-ahead walking. Since you look like the Incredible Hulk when you're running on the tread-mill, it is a good idea to spare the calories and use light mayonnaise.

Mix mayo, mustard, and relish in a bowl. When eggs have cooked, run them under cold water and peel. Chop eggs and combine with mayo mixture. Remember how your mother used to tell you that you'd grow out of it, how you tried yoga and Pilates and even got rolfed, all to no avail. Decide that you should get some extra-large pants and put padding in the inner thighs so that you just look really large legged. Or perhaps you could invest in a hat, boots, some spurs, and a horse and rent yourself out for children's parties. Sprinkle paprika on top of egg salad. Spread on bread and make two sandwiches: one for you and one for yer pardner.

STAYING TOGETHER FOR THE CHILDREN CHICKEN TETRAZZINI

You will need:

1 lb. spaghetti
½ lb. crimini mushrooms, sliced
1 stick butter
⅓ cup flour
Patience
1 large onion, sliced
4 cloves garlic, minced
1½ cups chicken broth
Hobbies
1 cup cream
1 large, soundproof box with
   padded walls and floor
¼ cup dry sherry
4 cups cubed chicken
1½ cups grated Parmesan cheese
Salt and pepper

Preheat oven to 400°F. While watching *Oprah*, cook and drain spaghetti according to package directions. Sauté mushrooms, onion, and garlic in 3 Tbs. butter until lightly browned. In a sauce pot, combine remaining butter, flour, and chicken broth, stirring over low heat until thickened. Add cream, sherry, salt, and pepper.

Start scrapbooking! Find favorite family photos and fill two books, one with colorful tags and funny little sayings over the photos and the other with the pictures just shoved in the sleeves. Put the second book in the box of stuff you are already packing for your husband when you finally get rid of him.

Mix sauce, chicken, and pasta in a large, buttered baking dish. Top with Parmesan cheese and bake for 20 minutes. In basement, shut yourself in soundproof box and scream. Scream again—a loud, primal scream that emanates from your very core—as you throw yourself against the padded walls until you are completely exhausted and can no longer stand.

Return to house proper and eat with children, before husband gets home, planting seeds of hatred and distrust in their tiny, impressionable heads while extolling your own many virtues. Leave small amount of tetrazzini for the bastard, on a plate on the counter, to dry out to a hard, rubbery mess. Wait in awkward silence for 2–18 years, depending on ages of children.

EL CHUPACABRA ATE ALL THE CHICKENS! CHIMICHANGA

You will need:

2 tortillas
Refried beans
Green chilies
Cheddar cheese
Oil for frying

Dios mío! You wake in the night and hear the terrible squawking of the chickens. You run outside to the henhouse. At first you can't see anything, so dark is the night. But then you see it! At first you see only the eyes. They are red and glowing. You think, "What is this, a monkey?" But you don't have monkeys here. Your cousin once had a monkey in his yard, but it turned out to be a neighbor's escaped pet. Then you think, "A dog?" But this is no dog. And then it occurs to you and you whisper out loud the name of the dreaded beast, "¡El *Chupacabra*!"

You run back into the house, knowing that the poor chickens are lost. You cannot fight the Chupacabra, and of course you are afraid for your own life. You remain awake the whole night, listening the flapping of wings as the Chupacabra drains the blood away from your chickens.

In the morning, when all is quiet, you return to the henhouse. There you find the lifeless bodies of your beloved *pollos*. All gone. You return to *su casa* and place some *frijoles refritos* on a tortilla, sprinkle on some green chilies and *queso*. You fold the tortilla over and fry it in oil until it is browned on both sides, and you eat it with some sour cream. Later, you go to the market and buy some more *pollos*.

CEREAL SNACK FOR AGING POTHEADS

You will need:

Cap'n Crunch
Milk
Chocolate syrup

Put down the grass, man, slip your stinky feet into some Birks, and go to the food co-op wearing as much patchouli oil as you can stand. While walking there, think about how the universe is completely aligned to bring you this totally far-out morning, and that each little bird is a creature with its own reality, living in time and in space, and that perhaps those little birds are just figments of your imagination, man. Whoa! Maybe other people's perception of those birds is totally different, like, when they see a bird, you know? Maybe when they see a bird it looks like a . . . like a . . . like a turtle, man! Or a Matchbox car! Kids are so cool. Also, think about how awesome Bugles corn chips are.

At the co-op, head straight for the cereal. Make sure to have a permanent smile plastered across your face and to say "Greetings, friend!" to those you pass in the aisles. Disdainfully regard anyone in a suit or anyone looking busy or productive. Then reconsider and give them your biggest smile. Tell them, "It's all good, my friend!"

Consider changing your name to Obadiah Earth Dolphin Phil Lesh Lovely Moonbeam.

Grab the Cap'n Crunch and tell the Cap'n, "Ahoy there, dude!" Bring him home and pour cereal into your favorite handmade pottery bowl; you know, the one that is sort of a puce color that you made while tripping on mescaline. That was some gnarly shit. Good times . . . yeah, good times.

Pour milk over cereal, and then pour on the chocolate syrup, anywhere from two squirts to the whole bottle. Enjoy cereal while listening to your *Sounds of the Rain Forest* CD to drown out the noise of the neighbor kids stealing your whirligigs.

Y OU SAW A GROUP OF GIRLS YOU WENT TO HIGH SCHOOL WITH AT A RESTAURANT AND YOU WERE THEIR WAITRESS CHIPOTLE BEANS AND RICE

You will need:

½ cup pinto beans
1 X-Acto knife
3 cups chicken stock
½ cup rice
1 tsp. canned chipotle
   chili in adobo sauce

Taking an old yearbook, carefully use X-Acto knife to slash photos of Lisa, Sophie, and Beth*. Leave Jeanne's face alone, as she was at least nice enough to leave a big tip, but the others deserve to be removed from the yearbook altogether, especially Lisa for the way she kept talking about how you were her "server" and then complained about not only the food but also your attitude. After removal from yearbook, use match to burn Lisa's photo.

Gently boil the beans in stock until almost soft. Add rice and chili and cook for 20–30 minutes until rice is tender. While cooking, consider working at a theme restaurant, like Planet Hollywood, because if someone you know shows up, it is an open question who should be more embarrassed. Enjoy beans with some hot sauce, if desired.

* Names have not been changed to protect now middle-age mean girls in humdrum lives.

OVING TO RUSSIA TO LOOK FOR WORK CHOCOBANBUTT PANINI

You will need:

Sweaters
Toilet paper
Jeans
Parka
Russian-language dictionary
Furry hat
Peanut butter
Banana
Chocolate hazelnut spread
2 slices white bread

"здравствйте, я здесь для того, чтобы цодать заявку на продаку пози-ции," which means, "Hello I am here to apply for the sales position!" or "What time does the duck tie his shoes?" Spread peanut butter on 1 slice of bread, chocolate on the other. Don't worry about the prohibitive cost of the chocolate spread—pretty soon you are likely to be earning a whopping fifteen thousand rubles a month! Never mind that that trans-lates roughly to $550, it's still more than you've brought home in the year since you were laid off.

Slice bananas and place on peanut butter. Enjoy fresh fruit now, because it is hard to come by in the Russian winter that lasts from mid-August to late July. Layer slices on top of one another and place in a small nonstick pan over high heat. Press down on top slice to squish flavors together and toast the bottom. Flip and repeat on the other side.

When both sides of panini are toasted, turn onto a plate. Enjoy as you learn how to say, "значит пи зто раьота включает прокие и питание?" which means, "Does this position include room and board?" If the an-swer is *nyet*, proceed with the following: "могу ли я слать в вашей кар-тоельный погреб?" or "May I sleep in your potato cellar?"

CINNAMON-SPICED APPLE FRITTER FOR WHEN YOUR HUSBAND RAN OFF WITH THE BABYSITTER

You will need:

2 apples
2 cups Bisquick
2/3 cup milk
1 egg
1 tsp. cinnamon
Oil for frying
Frumpy-looking nanny

Chop apples, roughly, leaving skins on. Wish that you had hired a rough-looking sitter instead of the beautiful blonde college student who watched your kids all summer. Mix together Bisquick, egg, and milk and stir in cinnamon.

Call mother of former babysitter to let her know that her daughter is a lying filthy home wrecker, and that she not only stole your husband but also your self-esteem and your favorite blue cashmere cardigan.

Drop apples in batter and stir to coat. Fry in oil until golden brown. On floor in living room, do Pilates, painful stomach crunches, push-ups, and squats, all in an effort to reverse direction of your sagging mommy's body. Collapse in exhaustion and frustration that you will never look as good as your husband's girlfriend.

In a large pot, heat oil to 360°F. Drop battered apples into hot oil, taking care not to splash any oil on your face, as hideous burn scars will not help you in your upcoming desperate search to find a mate.

Turn fritters and fry until golden brown. Since children are closer in age to the babysitter than you are, they will likely need to be *told* why they should hate her. Compile a list of reasons for them, including lies, if necessary:

> She wants to send them to a school in the mountains where they
>   will have to forage for food.
> She will spend their college funds buying fur coats.
> She belongs to a cult that regularly sacrifices puppies and children.
> She is German.

Sprinkle fritters with powdered sugar and enjoy as your last meal before the breast enhancement.

CHICKEN TERIYAKI FOR WHEN YOUR CAREER IN ADVERTISING HAS DESTROYED YOUR SOUL

You will need:

1 lb. Purdue Tender and
  Tasty chicken tenders
1 cup flour
2 eggs
1 cup new-and-
  improved milk
1 red pepper, sliced
1 onion, sliced
¼ cup pineapple chunks,
  if desired
6 Tbs. purchased teriyaki
  sauce, now with no MSG!
2 Tbs. oil

Where's the beef? Not here; we're making chicken! Take *the incredible edible egg* and crack two into a bowl. *Got milk?* Pour it in with the eggs. Put flour in a separate bowl. *I'm a pepper, you're a pepper, wouldn't you like to* put some pepper into the flour? Then do it! Put in some . . . *Can you hear me now? Good.* Put in some salt too. Dredge chicken in eggs, then in flour. *Time to make the donuts*—I mean, rice! Cook rice according to package directions. Heat oil in a skillet, and then *plop plop, fizz fizz* the chicken into the oil. Add red pepper, onion, and teriyaki sauce and cook for 10 minutes or . . . *Can you hear me now? Good.* Cook until chicken is done.

Add pineapple and cook for 1 more minute, being careful . . . *Can you hear me now? Good* (that's enough of that). Being careful not to slip on any egg that might have fallen on the floor or you'll find that *you've fallen and you can't get up. You deserve a break today,* but not that kind of break! Think to yourself, "*I wish I were an Oscar Mayer wiener* or a bricklayer or a plumber, or anything other than a soulless ad exec. I should have been a playwright." Serve teriyaki over rice, being careful not to *squeeze the Charmin*. Hang head in shame.

**ANIC-DEPRESSIVE BROWNIES, TWO WAYS!**

THE MANIC WAY

You will need:

2 sticks butter
8 oz. bittersweet chocolate
1 cup dark brown sugar
1 cup sugar
2 tsp. vanilla
4 eggs
1 cup flour
½ tsp. salt

Eat Your Feelings

At 3:00 a.m., butter a 13 × 9 inch dish. Cut parchment paper to exact dimensions of dish, being careful not to cut yourself with scissors due to shaky hands. If hands are too shaky for this task, run around your block five or six times to try to settle down. Butter parchment and place it in pan.

Preheat oven to 350°F. Check oven temperature every fifteen seconds until desired temperature is reached, hopping from one foot to the other and periodically bursting into fits of uncontrollable laughter.

Place water in bottom of a double boiler and bring to a simmer. If you do not have a double boiler, place a metal bowl over a pot of simmering water. When water is near boiling, stick your finger in it just to see how much it hurts. Do it again, and time yourself to see how long you can stand it. Melt butter with chocolate in the top of double boiler.

Call people on phone. When nobody answers, call friends in Sweden, folks who work on farms, and finally the Home Shopping Network. Buy six or seven of every item, just to keep them on the line.

In a separate bowl, crack eggs one at a time. Try to focus yourself for a minute to see if any eggshells fell into the bowl. If they did, get really mad at yourself and the eggs; then fish them out with your fingers and wipe hands on pants. Whisk in sugars, salt, and vanilla.

Fold in chocolate mixture amid growing feelings of grandiosity, admiring the swift and masterly way your wrist controls the whisk. You could be a pastry chef—as a matter of fact, if you *were* a pastry chef, you would probably be a world famous baker like . . . you would be the *first ever* world famous baker!

Pour batter into prepared baking dish and bake for 35 minutes or until glistening.

THE DEPRESSIVE WAY

You will need:

1 box brownie mix
1 egg
$\frac{2}{3}$ cup oil

Eat Your Feelings

Don't bother to preheat oven; you're not going to get that far. Combine brownie mix with egg and oil, stirring until you just can't bring yourself to stir any longer. What's the point? We're all alone in an uncaring universe, essentially just killing time until we die. Probably, there's something just waiting to kill you right now. Perhaps it is the raw egg you are about to eat.

Using a large spoon, eat mix right out of bowl. Recognize your own worthlessness, using as examples the fact that you are sitting on the floor in the dark, in the same pajamas you've been wearing for three days, and the large bowl of batter in your lap.

$\mathcal{P}$OSTPARTUM POTATO PIEROGIES

You will need:

Shampoo
Soap
Clean clothes
1 box frozen potato pierogies
Sour cream
Applesauce
1 onion
Butter

Eat Your Feelings

It's been three months since you forced an eight pounder into the world through your ravaged vaginal tract. You haven't showered in a month, and in that time you've eaten nothing but lousy TV dinners brought home to you by your baby's useless father. Oh, and the occasional spoonful of chocolate syrup. It's pierogi time!

Making pierogies is an extremely time-consuming process, and Lord knows you don't have the energy or fortitude for such a task. Luckily, frozen pierogies are available almost everywhere, and they are good enough for a depressive slob like you.

First things first: Strap baby into car seat or bouncy chair; stick it in a drawer, if you must—whatever you have to do to take a shower, because you stink. Make sure to scrub clumps of dried spit-up from back of hair. And use soap. Please.

After shower, put on clean clothes. It wouldn't hurt to brush your hair either. Also, a little eyeliner goes a long way. Remove hospital ID bracelet.

Slice onion very thin and fry in butter over low heat. Add pierogies to pan and cook until nice and brownish. Serve with applesauce and sour cream; realize the baby isn't going to cry itself to death if you put her down for a minute while you enjoy a glass of wine and dream about nannies and boarding school.

*M*IL FROM HELL TACO BELL

You will need:

Car

Eat Your Feelings

When your mother-in-law plops herself down in front of your computer to play Sudoku for hours at a time, do not bristle. When your mother-in-law forages through your refrigerator, pay no attention. When she asks you to make her a tuna sandwich, do so with a smile. When your mother-in-law extols the virtues of your husband's ex-wife, saying that her tuna sandwiches were "exquisite," do not shove said sandwich in her face.

When your mother-in-law tells your child that it is a pity he doesn't have a mommy like her, pretend not to hear. When your mother-in-law has fourth crying jag in one day, complaining that your husband just doesn't love her anymore, hand her the stinking tissues. When your mother-in-law falls asleep on the couch in the middle of the afternoon, get in the car.

Head for nearest Taco Bell and order:

  1 Spicy Chicken Crunchwrap Supreme
  1 Gordita Baja
  1 Chalupa Nacho Cheese
  1 side Cheesy Fiesta Potatoes
  1 large Mountain Dew Baja Blast
  2 orders Cinnamon Twists

Eat while sitting in car, taking as much time as needed to remind yourself why you put up with her: not because your children love their grandma, but for her house in Nantucket.

EMERGENCY FOOD SOURCE FOR PLANE-CRASH SURVIVORS

You will need:

Confidence
Quick thinking
Patience
Sharp object

This recipe is, as stated, only for *emergencies* and not to be used if your plane has crashed on, say, an island with lots of food sources or some-place where there is access to grocery stores.

First move the bodies of the deceased to a cool area. This is easier if you have crashed on a mountain or near a polar ice cap. Next you must quickly assign blame for the crash. The easiest person to blame is the pilot. But as *you are* the pilot, you need to quickly point the finger else-where; wear your pilot's hat for extra gravitas. Tell the other survivors that the copilot smelled like alcohol, and that you knew he had a problem but you didn't know how bad it was till now.

You will also need to ingratiate yourself with the other survivors. Some of them may be complaining (there may be bone fractures, gashes, whiplash, or missed connections); some may have tedious personalities; some will just be jerks. No matter! You must make them like you, and to do that you have to listen to them and—this is *very important*— you have to *empathize* with them or at least make them think that you do. Without this crucial step, you risk mutiny.

Once people start to get hungry, it's time to make some hard decisions. The first is *who to eat*. This is why it was a good idea to assign blame: That person is first up on the chopping block.

Using sharp object, find the fattiest portion of the corpse and carve out some nice-size fillets, one for each survivor. It isn't really going to be pos-sible to cook the fillets, but if there is a lens available, for example, from a severely myopic passenger, you can use it to focus sunlight onto the steaks and give them a nice sear. Repeat as often as necessary until res-cue, or until you run out of people to blame. Then you're on your own.

CAUGHT MOM AND DAD IN THE ACT TATER TOT CASSEROLE

You will need:

1 package Tater Tots
1 can condensed cream of mushroom soup
1 16 oz. container sour cream
1 cup shredded cheddar cheese
¼ cup shredded Monterey Jack cheese
1 can french-fried onions
Paprika

Preheat oven to 350°F. In a bowl, combine sour cream, half of cheese, and mushroom soup, realizing it is the same grayish brown color as your father's naked behind. Suppress memory. Grease bottom of a large baking dish. Arrange Tater Tots in a single layer on bottom of dish, the way your mom was laying spread-eagle underneath your father.

Pour soup mixture over Tots, trying to convince yourself that it is sweet that they are still attracted to each other at this advanced age. As thinking of their advanced age brings to mind their sagging nether regions, vomit in your mouth. Brush teeth until fully convinced parents are perverted sex fiends.

Spread remaining cheese over casserole, sprinkle with paprika, and bake for 45 minutes to 1 hour, until golden and bubbling. Eat casserole while making upcoming holiday plans that do not involve parents, as eating around them is now impossible.

A LOPECIA PIZZA

You will need:

Pizza crust
Mozzarella cheese, shredded
Fontina cheese, shredded
Parmesan cheese, shredded
Ricotta cheese
Olive oil
Pepper

Preheat oven to 500°F. Roll out dough to a round pizza shape, about the same diameter as the full moon or your head. In the same way that you have been dabbing Rogaine on your bald cranium for the past year (to no avail), drizzle olive oil over dough and top with dabs of ricotta.

Take handful of shredded cheese and sprinkle it on dough, much like the handfuls of hair you pull out in the shower, and exactly like the hair that falls out all over your home, office, car, and any other place you happen to be when a mild breeze or fan is blowing.

Season with pepper and more olive oil, and bake for 10–15 minutes or until crust is baked and cheese melted. Do not attempt to place pizza on scalp to cover baldness, as it will burn more than the hair-regrowth serum you bought at the Amish market. Just eat it and be thankful that you still have your eyebrows. For now.

OM'S OLD-FASHIONED CHICKEN NOODLE SOUP FOR CLOSET CASES

You will need:

8 cups chicken broth
½ chicken, in pieces
1 small onion, chopped
2 carrots, washed or scrubbed
(depending on what you've
done with them) and
thinly sliced
2 stalks of celery, sliced
1 Tbs. butter (not Boy Butter,
actual butter)
1 cup sliced mushrooms
1 squeeze fresh lemon juice
8 oz. wide egg noodles
½ cup fresh parsley
¼ cup fresh dill

Place broth and chicken into a large pot like the one you found last summer, with your wife, at that fabulous little flea market in Amagansett. Bring to a boil. Place the lid at a jaunty angle on top to let off some steam and simmer until the chicken is cooked, about 20 minutes or just enough time to do your Buns of Steel workout routine.

Take chicken out and put it into a bowl. Use years of practiced tough-guy behavior to remove skin and bones, and tear the meat into bite-sized pieces. Skim fat off broth. Yuck!

Turn up the heat on the broth, like you would love to turn up the heat with your brother-in-law Ted with his skinny jeans and plump little—*get it together*. Add carrots, onions, and celery to the broth. Simmer until they, and you, become soft.

Practice masculine walking, wearing sneakers or, better yet, Timberland boots. Practice saying "bro" and "dude," and brush up on your sports stats.

Cook mushrooms in butter. When they start to brown, add lemon juice. Then add them to the pot, licking your fingers and pretending to be Nigella Lawson. Stir in egg noodles, herbs, and chicken. Season with salt and pepper, and lament the fact that "fantasy football" isn't at all what you thought it was.

YOU GOT DRUNK AND CALLED YOUR FRIEND A SLUT IN FRONT OF HER FATHER CHEESEBURGER SOUP

You will need:

4 potatoes, cooked and cubed
1 onion, sliced
1 lb. ground beef
1 pack white American cheese
2 cups chicken stock (or as needed)

In a skillet, brown beef and pour off fat. Cook onion until soft. Phone florist and order one large bouquet for your friend and one for her dad. Pray nobody else heard you: Flowers are expensive.

Put onion and potatoes into blender, adding stock gradually until desired consistency is reached. Pour into a pot. Bring to a low boil and simmer, you know, like the rage in your friend's father's eyes as he shoved you into a taxi at his annual Fourth of July party. Apply bacitracin to the wounds on your heels from when you dug them into the driveway, screaming that you weren't going anywhere until that slut apologized to you. Add ground beef and cheese, stirring until cheese is melted.

Replay events of the evening in your mind. You'd had a few drinks and gone to splash some cold water on your face. That's when you found her in the bathtub with, not one, not two, but three of the waiters *and* her cousin—the one *you* were flirting with earlier. She's lucky you didn't call the police.

Phone florist to cancel her flowers, but have them send the bouquet to her dad. After all, it's not entirely his fault that his daughter is a complete whore, and, even if it is, he throws a great party, with an open bar, and you want to be invited back.

PERFECT MASHED POTATOES FOR DISAPPOINTED PARENTS

You will need:

Potatoes
Cream
Butter
Salt
Pepper

Peel potatoes and cut into quarters. Rinse potatoes as you drain away any previously held hopes for the success of your child. Throw peels in garbage along with all college applications. You won't be needing those, as your child has been thrown out of every school he ever attended, beginning with Little Rainbows Nursery School straight through to the work-study High School Equivalency Program.

Put potatoes in a large pot and cover with water. Potatoes will sink to the bottom of the pot much like your son, who, when you took him to swimming lessons, and no matter how hard they tried to teach him, sank to the bottom every time. Recall with vivid embarrassment how the instructor explained that your son had a complete lack of athletic ability, as well as an inability to close his mouth, even underwater.

Boil until potatoes are tender. Drain and rinse, the way you rinsed your hands of all responsibility when he was caught taking puppies from the local animal shelter and setting them on fire.

Return potatoes to pot and add cream and butter. Take out years of pent-up desire to throttle your son on the potatoes and mash them to a smooth consistency. Pour gin. Drink. Realize son has replaced gin with water.

Season with salt and pepper. Enjoy while accustoming yourself to idea that while most children leave home after twenty years, yours isn't going anywhere. Ever. Consider taking up smoking to get it over with quicker.

B AD BOTOX BOLOGNESE

You will need:

1 rib celery
1 carrot
1 onion
2 Tbs. olive oil
18 oz. ground beef
3 cloves garlic, minced
½ cup white wine
2 cans whole plum tomatoes,
   in their juice
⅓ cup milk

Eat Your Feelings

Finely chop celery, carrot, and onion the way you had your eye bags finely chopped off your face last year. Heat oil in a large pot over a medium-high flame. Do not attempt to save money on silicone by injecting oil into face, as it will lead to excessive plumping. Add beef and chopped vegetables and sauté for 8 minutes or until softened; then add garlic and cook for 2 minutes more. Lifts hands to physically feel if tears are falling. If so, apply tissue so as not to add tears to pot.

Add wine and simmer for 10 minutes. In your condition you cannot assume that people will be able to read your emotions on your face, so use this time to practice verbal expression of feelings. For example, "my dog died" must now become, "I am so terribly distraught that my beloved dog has died. I will miss him so much. I really, *really* loved my dog, and now he has died." Likewise, "I'm really angry" must now become, "I'm so freaking pissed off at you right now that I am on the verge of ripping your head off. Take a good look at this frozen, paralyzed, wrinkle-free face, as it will be the last thing you ever see." Add milk to pot and simmer for an additional 5 minutes.

Add tomatoes, squishing between your fingers to break them up. Leave to simmer for 45 minutes while you figure out what to do about those annoying knee bags. To eat pasta, tilt head back, open mouth, and shovel in noodles, using fingers to hold mouth closed while chewing. Bib suggested.

Y OU WERE A BULLY IN MIDDLE SCHOOL BANANA BREAD

You will need:

1 stick butter
1 cup sugar
2 eggs
1½ cups flour
1 tsp. baking soda
1 tsp. salt
1½ cups mashed ripe bananas
½ cup plain yogurt
1 tsp. vanilla
Extra butter and sugar

Eat Your Feelings

Butter inside of loaf pan and coat with sugar; just like you coated the outside of Laurie Johnson's locker with Crisco in eighth grade. That was a riot. Cream together butter and sugar, and add eggs. Remember the day you put the CREAMED MY JEANS sign on Danny Doyle's back. Awesome.

Mix together flour, baking soda, and salt, and add to butter. Mix until blended. What was the name of that girl you used to kick in the stairwell after chemistry in seventh grade? Put the bananas, yogurt, and vanilla into the mix, and stir while you try to remember. She was short and had glasses. Hmm . . . Tracy? Maybe. What a loser. Decide to look her up online. Find a recent news article, "Tracy McGillicuddy Elected to Third Term in U.S. Senate"? What the . . .

Call upstairs to your mother to ask if you can use the oven. If she says yes, preheat it to 350°F. Pour batter into the loaf pan and bake for 1 hour. Take bread out of the oven, dot with additional butter, and sprinkle the top with sugar. Bake for an additional 10 minutes or until done. Invite neighbor-kid over for banana bread and stick his head in the toilet.

YOUR MARRIAGE IS A DISASTER SICILIAN LASAGNA

You will need:

½ package lasagna noodles
1 lb. ground beef
1 onion, chopped
1 pint ricotta cheese
2 eggs
12 oz. tomato paste
1 clove garlic, minced
1 cup water
1 Tbs. salt
2 Tbs. dried rosemary
1 cup shredded
   mozzarella cheese
¼ cup grated Parmesan
1 cup pharmaceutical atropine,
   ground*

Eat Your Feelings

Preheat oven to 350°F. Sweep up shards of broken glass and grandmother's china from last night's argument. Bring large pot of salted water to a boil and cook noodles according to package directions. In a large pan (perhaps the one you hit your spouse over the head with the last time he called you a stupid cow and mooed at you every time you asked him something), brown beef with onion.

Meanwhile beat together ricotta and eggs, pouring anger, frustration, and tendency toward violence into the mixture. Remember that hubby stole ten thousand dollars from your grandmother to spend on Vicodin. Beat harder.

Rummage through his drawers until you find irrefutable evidence that he is sleeping with your sister. It should be in his sock drawer, under all the gay porn, and in the form of naked photos of the two of them together. Note with a modicum of surprise that the other person in the photos is your brother.

Back in the kitchen, add atropine powder to cheese mix, being careful not to taste or ingest in any way, as it will cause death. In a small pot, over low heat, combine water, tomato paste, garlic, and rosemary.

When noodles are fully cooked, assemble the lasagna in a 13 × 9 inch baking dish in layers as follows:

> Small amount of sauce
> ½ of noodles
> ½ of sauce
> Ricotta-bitterness mix
> Rest of noodles
> Meat for the meathead you married

Rest of sauce

Mozzarella

Parmesan

Sprinkle the finished lasagna with leftover atropine. Bake for 45 minutes or until brown and bubbling. Place on table set with flowers and wine, with a little note just saying, "Sorry." Perhaps draw a cute smiley face to discourage suspicion.

* Atropine, while not readily available in grocery stores, can be obtained with a prescription or by robbing a pharmacy. In remote areas, it is possible to make atropine from scratch if enough deadly nightshade is available.

YOU ARE GOING TO [VERB] [PERSON] FOR [ADVERB] [VERB] YOUR [NOUN] TWICE-BAKED POTATOES

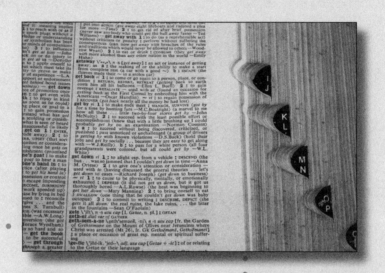

You will need:

[Noun]
2 large baking potatoes
Coarse salt
¼ cup shredded cheddar cheese
2 Tbs. sour cream
2 tsp. chives, chopped
2 Tbs. bacon bits

Preheat oven to 400°F. Call _____ (person) on phone and tell them their _____ (thing) is _____ (adjective), and that they can shove their _____ (thing) up their _____ (adjective) _____ (place) until it _____ (verb). Wash potatoes thoroughly, then dry and roll in coarse salt the way that _____ (person) rubbed salt in your _____ (place). Poke holes all over potatoes the way _____ (person] poked holes all over your _____ (thing). Bake in oven for 45 minutes or until done.

Cut potatoes in half and scoop out flesh. Mix potato flesh with sour cream and chives, season with salt and pepper, and spoon back into skins. Go next door and discreetly borrow neighbor's _____ (thing) and use it to _____ (verb) _____ (person), making sure not to leave _____ (things) on the _____ (thing). Return _____ (thing) to neighbor. Top potatoes with cheddar cheese and return to oven. Bake for 5–7 minutes or until cheese is melted. Sprinkle on bacon bits and enjoy while you _____ (verb) your _____ (noun) to convince _____ (person) that you are _____ (adjective). Clean up _____ (noun).

LITTLE SISTER EARNS MORE THAN YOU HAM AND CHEESE TOASTIE

You will need:

2 slices crusty bread
Ham
Cheese
Butter

Butter tops of bread the way your little sister buttered up each and every teacher she had in high school. Place ham on top of bread—this will bring to mind what a ham she was in the school play. In fact, nobody has ever played Rizzo with quite so much gusto. Wonder when people in town are going to stop saying, "Oh, your sister is Tracy? She was *so* wonderful in *Grease!*" You gave a really honest and subtle performance as Principal McGee. You didn't need to belt out those crappy songs just to get attention. And it's much harder to play an old woman when you're a senior in high school than it is to play a senior in high school when you're a junior in high school. Everybody knows that. Place cheese on top of ham.

Call little sister at work. When her assistant says she is unavailable, tell him that it is an emergency. When Tracy gets on the phone, do not bristle at the way she only says her last name instead of hello like a normal person. Calmly remind her that you scored eighty points higher than she did on the verbal SAT and hang up the phone.

Place bread on a piece of aluminum foil in a toaster oven. Begin to worry about Christmas. Do not allow a repeat of last year, when she gave everyone a trip to Europe and you gave everyone soap on a rope. Call parents and implement a secret-Santa policy with a twenty-dollar spending limit.

Broil in toaster oven until cheese is melted and bubbling. Enjoy with a tall glass of humiliation.

H E ONLY MARRIED YOU FOR HIS GREEN CARD CHICKEN SALAD

You will need:

2½ cups cooked chicken, cubed
1 cup diced celery
½ cup diced onion
1 cup chopped grapes
⅓ cup mayonnaise
1 Tbs. red wine vinegar
1 tsp. dried tarragon
Air mattresses or spare cots

Push past your husband's brothers, the ones who seem to be suddenly living in your hallway, to get to the kitchen. Using hand gestures and speaking loudly, ask his grandmother if it would be okay for you to use your kitchen counter, where she has been preparing some sort of fried dumpling thing that takes four days to ferment. Place cubed chicken in a large bowl. Add chopped celery, onion, and grapes.

In a separate bowl, mix mayonnaise with red wine vinegar, if you can wrestle it away from his uncle who seems to rub it on his feet to purify his soul or remove warts.

Pause to look at wedding photos of a much happier version of yourself. Recall that you thought you had met the man of your dreams: tall, handsome, and seemingly in love with you. Wish your husband didn't refer to your anniversary as "the day of escape from the fascist regime" and insist on celebrating by jumping through a bonfire in your driveway. Eye the mysterious "cousin" who glares at you, muttering what sounds like curses under her breath. What is her deal anyway? Maybe she's just cranky because she's pregnant.

Mix tarragon into mayonnaise and pour dressing over chicken, tossing to coat. Take bowl to rooftop to eat in peace before realizing you haven't seen your cat in three days.

STIR-FRY FOR STRETCH MARKS

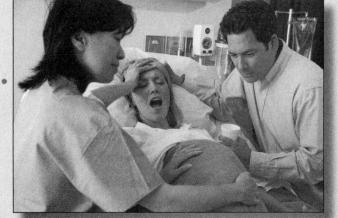

You will need:

2 Tbs. oil
1 red pepper
1 cup snow peas
1 cup broccoli florets
2 boneless, skinless chicken breasts
½ onion
Old-lady bathing suit
1 cup hoisin sauce

Slice onion and peppers into thin strips. While it is true that if you were to cut thin strips off your abdomen and thighs you wouldn't have the stretch marks, do not do so! It is extremely dangerous and painful! Heat oil in a wok or large skillet, being careful not to scald flabby, nonelastic skin. Keep in mind that burn marks are no better than stretch marks and the two together are pretty messy.

In a large bowl, combine chicken, vegetables, and sauce. Toss to coat. Rub stir-fry sauce on problem area in an attempt to realize an as yet undiscovered treatment for stretch marks. If yours are as the result of pregnancy, do not blame or take frustration out on children, even though it is technically their fault.

Place all ingredients in wok and fry for 15 minutes, stirring often, until chicken is fully cooked. Enjoy over rice while you practice telling others that you view your stretch marks as a "badge of honor," even though nobody will believe you.

$\mathcal{L}$ONELY CHRISTMAS PUDDING

You will need:

1 Christmas tree
Christmas music
1 box gingerbread or spice cake mix
1 can pumpkin
¼ cup butter
¼ cup confectioner's sugar
1 bottle brandy, any quality, doesn't matter

Put on Christmas music. Preheat oven to 350°F. Grease a Bundt pan. Prepare cake mix according to package directions, substituting canned pumpkin for egg and oil. Under the Christmas tree, find the solitary present you wrapped for yourself. Open and change into those new pajamas—just what you wanted! Pour batter into the pan and bake for 35 minutes or until done.

To prepare hard sauce, mix softened butter with brandy and sugar to taste. Oh, and you better taste the brandy. Then taste brandy again, just to be sure. No need to bother with a glass—nobody's here anyway.

Remove cake from oven, douse with brandy, slather with hard sauce, and enjoy with more brandy.

Turn on television just for the sound of the voices. Drink brandy until you fall asleep, comforted by the thought that when you wake up it won't be Christmas anymore.

HARDTACK FOR LONELY SEAMEN ON WHALING VESSELS

Ye will be needin':

4 cups flour
4 tsp. salt
2 cups rainwater

For the times betwixt the spottin' of the great fish and the oily material wherewith, this recipe is mighty good for fixin' ye some hardtack to quiet the rumblin' o' the tummy whilst ye are achin' for the love of your lassie.

Stir up the flour and the salt while the ship be layin' still so as not to cause the mixture to spill or be blowin' off in the hard wind. Mix in the water, stirrin' it around with the swiftness of a gale, till the paste be not a-stickin' to the hands. Roll out the dough to resemble a tablet, smooth like the sea in a dead calm, anon piercing it with your fingers as ye would a whale's blubbery sides with a harpoon.

After the dough is rolled flat like a sail on a windless morn, shape into a rectangle and cut into squares, 3 inches by 3 inches, or exactly the size of the cap'n's boot buckle.

With a bit of scrimshaw fashioned to a point, press into the dough a pattern of a whale or a maiden blowin' a horn, but use a gentle hand, not to punch through, but just to press into the dough as ye would dip the rudder in the briny sea. Do this on both sides as ye like, mayhap puttin' in the likeness of your lassie's countenance on the aft side; then bake in an oven set to the temperature of 375°F. After 30 minutes, or the amount of time it takes to cleave the pieces of the monster in the blubber room to yield the whale oil, take the hardtack out o' the oven and eat forthwith.

LEFT AT THE ALTAR PETITS-FOURS LOG

You will need:

Receipts

Linger at the altar no longer than 10 minutes. Be sure when leaving to storm straight down the aisle, not looking at anyone. You have two roles to consider: the poor, heartbroken bride or the angry, vengeful bride. I would opt for heartbroken, as your guests may not expect their gifts to be returned if they feel sorry for you.

Do not take off dress, no matter how uncomfortable you become, as wearing a wedding dress entitles you to order people around. In back of the church or reception hall, demand bridesmaids bring you all the lovely little cakes you and your bastard fiancé spent eighteen months picking out. Send maid of honor to fetch three bottles of champagne.

Take all petits fours and squash them into two log shapes, imagining they're your fiancé's face. When the maid of honor arrives with champagne, open one bottle and drink. Glass unnecessary. When mother of the groom arrives to offer sympathy, throw empty bottle at her, being careful to miss her head, as nobody will feel sorry for you anymore if you kill her.

Screaming in a loud voice, tell everyone that you want them to "*Leave!*" If necessary, push or shove them out of the room, including your closest friends and family members. Turn attention to the gifts. Tear open packages and sort contents into two piles, one for keeping and one for returning. Be sure to keep any gift receipts included with the returns.

Eat second petits-fours log, and tell everyone you know that fiancé would only have sex with you if you wore a blindfold and called him Boss Hog, being sure to elicit additional sympathy by pretending this was confusing and disturbing to you.

PEPPERONI PIZZA FOR AGORAPHOBES

You will need:

1 package dry yeast
1 cup lukewarm water
Pinch of sugar
1 tsp salt
3–3½ cups white flour
Phone

The year was 1994. O. J. Simpson was driving the California freeway in his Bronco, the soundtrack from the motion picture *The Bodyguard* topped the charts, and thousands of flannel-clad grungies mourned the loss of Kurt Cobain. It was also the last time you left the house. You've been getting by on frozen dinners, but now you have a hankering for some fresh pizza.

Put yeast in a warm bowl and pour in water and sugar. Mix well with a fork and leave until yeast starts to foam, about 5–10 minutes. (Leave the mixture—you don't actually have to *leave the house*, no need to panic just yet.)

Using a wooden spoon, add salt and about ⅔ of the flour, stirring until dough comes away from sides of the bowl. Sprinkle some of the remaining flour onto a smooth surface and kneed dough, adding a little flour at a time until it is elastic. In the approximately 10 minutes this should take, mentally prepare yourself for procuring pizza toppings. Use tapping therapy, gently knocking on the backs of your hand, on your brow bone, and on your collarbone while you think about how freaked out you'll be when you have to meet the delivery guy from the grocery store.

Put dough in a lightly oiled mixing bowl and cover with a damp towel. Leave in a warm place for about an hour.

Phone grocery store and ask them to deliver:

1 can pizza sauce
1 package shredded mozzarella
1 pepperoni

Eat Your Feelings

Have at the ready:

1 can opener
1 large ziplock bag
1 paper bag

When deliveryman arrives, brace your back against the wall to steady yourself, as the floor will appear to be dropping out from under you. While tapping vigorously on your collarbone, yell through door at delivery guy to put cheese and pepperoni through the mail slot. When the items are safely inside, quickly pass can opener and ziplock bag through the mail slot and instruct the delivery person to open can, squeeze tomato sauce into plastic bag, and pass it back to you through the slot. If delivery man is uncooperative, shout, "Just *do it*, man!" over and over, all the while tapping under your eyes with increasing vigor, until he complies. Place paper bag over mouth and nose, and inhale deeply to control hyperventilation.

Preheat oven to 475°F. Stretch or roll dough into a pizzalike shape. Spread sauce over top and cover with cheese and pepperoni. Bake until bubbling, about 15 minutes. Ice collarbone to avoid bruising. Cut pizza into quarters. If delivery man is still outside waiting for a tip, slide one slice of pizza out to him. Assume he'll find his own napkin.

RELUCTANT BREADWINNER'S QUICHE FOR RESENTFUL WIVES OF STAY-AT-HOME DADS

You will need:

1 whole-wheat piecrust
6 eggs
2/3 cup heavy cream
1 cup milk
Large hunk of Swiss cheese, grated
1 onion
1 Tbs. butter

Rush home from soul-destroying but well-paying job to spend time with your children. Find husband chatting with mommies on urbanbaby.com while children watch *Noggin*. Give dirty look to husband. When he says, "What? Dora enhances children's language skills and interpersonal relationships," give him a second dirty look. When he turns back to the computer to tell his online mommy friends how controlling and judgmental you are, give him a swat to the back of the head.

In kitchen, poke holes in piecrust and preheat oven to 425°F. Line crust with aluminum foil and fill with dried beans or pie weights. Bake in oven for 15 minutes or until golden brown. Slice onion into paper-thin rounds and ask yourself why you married a man who claimed to be an artist but never really created anything. Ask yourself why that didn't occur to you *before* you had three children. Sauté onion in butter, over low heat, until golden and caramelized.

Beat together eggs, cream, and milk. Season with salt and pepper. When husband announces he has a "gig" as a DJ at a bar mitzvah next weekend, just ignore it. Grate cheese and spread it around piecrust. Top with onions. Place crust on a baking sheet to avoid spills in the oven—Lord knows, you'll have to clean it up yourself. Enjoy brief fantasy of husband cooking and cleaning, wearing an apron, and handing you a cocktail when you walk in the door. Snap back to reality when he tells you he needs a little "mad money" because he's having lunch with the ladies from Baby Yoga tomorrow. Think that if you had known you would be the sole breadwinner for a family of five, you might have majored in economics or math rather than anthropology with a minor in theater arts.

Realize that if you had not minored in theater arts, you might never have met your husband. Sigh.

Pour eggs over onion and cheese, and bake for 30 minutes or until filling is baked through. If crust gets too brown, cover edges with aluminum foil and continue baking until done. Enjoy with several glasses of wine and irritation.

REJECTED BY SKIDMORE AND THAT WAS YOUR SAFETY SCHOOL CHICKEN FRIED STEAK

You will need:

2 5-inch skirt steaks
1 cup beef broth
2 cups flour
¼ stick butter
Salt and pepper

Season steaks with salt and pepper. Pour broth into one bowl and flour into another. Compose letters to *perfidious* social studies teacher and guidance counselor who were supposed to write you great recommendations and obviously didn't—because everyone knows you are a *superlative* student and an excellent candidate for Skidmore. (Everyone except Skidmore, that is.)

Make preemptive, face-saving strike by composing a letter rescinding your applications to as yet unresponsive colleges and universities. Mark all Skidmore paraphernalia, including mugs and sweatshirts, for your mother's next yard sale.

Dredge steaks in flour, swish them in broth in a *circuitous* manner, and then dredge in flour again. Next dredge out your high school transcript and try to figure out what the hell happened. Consider resigning from the National Honor Society, which clearly means about as much as your position as treasurer of the Orienteering Club.

Without becoming *querulous*, call admissions office at Skidmore. Ask to speak with the dean. When dean is unavailable, ask the receptionist if they realized that you have been on both the Science Olympiad team and the lacrosse team (and *not* JV, by the way). Hang up when she asks for your name. Who does she think she is anyway? Some sort of *plenipotentiary*?

Melt butter in skillet over high heat, add steaks, and *cauterize* until browned. Put away SAT vocabulary study guide: It's too late for that now. Enjoy with gravy, if desired, and arrange a trip out of town for your first "semester," perhaps a job with a traveling Renaissance Faire. Refer to college as stifling to your creativity.

YOUR BIRTHDAY IS SEPTEMBER 11
CHOCOLATE MUD CAKE

You will need:

4 oz. unsweetened chocolate,
 chopped
3 oz. best-quality bittersweet chocolate, chopped
1½ sticks butter
1½ cups brewed coffee
5 Tbs. bourbon
2 eggs
1 tsp. vanilla
2 cups cake flour
1¾ cups sugar
1 tsp. baking soda
¼ tsp. salt
Dash cinnamon
Cups of liquid
Invitations

SOME TIPS FOR THE PARTY

Begin two weeks prior to birthday by sending out invitations printed as follows:

Please come for a party to celebrate my birthday!
Where: My house!
When: Second Saturday in September

Do not mention the date or the numbers nine or eleven. Remove all calendars and other indicators of date/month from your home. In fact, avoid the decade in question altogether and make it a seventies theme party and play disco music!

Do not hold the party between 9:00 and 10:00 a.m., to avoid those respectful yet awkward moments of silence.

Place cups of liquid randomly throughout house.

No flags! In fact, there should be as little to remind people of what country they are in as possible. That means rethinking your "America the Great" decorative plate set.

Do not talk about firemen or fire, and refrain from using the words "finest" or "bravest."

Good topics for conversation are other days in September. Try, "Labor Day is also in September. Labor Day is great!"

If the tragedy should come up in conversation, quickly grab nearest cup of liquid and spill it on somebody.

Be sure to open presents first, just in case the mood turns. Don't forget to tell people how safe and secure they are and, whatever you do, don't mention Osama bin Laden.

FOR THE CAKE

Preheat oven to 275°F. Butter two 8-inch springform pans, line with parchment paper, and dust with flour. In a large pot, melt chocolate with butter and coffee—make sure the coffee is extra strong to keep people peppy! Stir constantly until smooth. Remove from heat for 10 minutes while you practice disco moves.

Beat in bourbon, eggs, and vanilla, then sift in flour, sugar, baking soda, salt, and cinnamon. Stir until smooth and divide between pans, then bake for 1 hour or until cake tester comes out with bits of cake gently adhering to it. Turn onto a wire rack to cool before frosting with bright, cheerful colors (avoid red, white, and blue).

IT'S TIME TO SETTLE SPAGHETTI CARBONARA FOR WOMEN IN THEIR "THIRTIES"

You will need:

- 1 lb. spaghetti
- 4 slices bacon
- 2 cloves garlic, sliced
- 2 eggs
- ½ cup Parmesan cheese
- 1 Tbs. chopped fresh parsley

Cook bacon in a large skillet until crisp. Pour off most of fat and sauté garlic. If drinking wine while cooking, do not send "sexy" text message to your ex. Neither he nor his frustratingly younger new girlfriend will appreciate the interruption.

Cook spaghetti in a large pot of boiling salted water until *al dente*, as you have done many, *many* lonely nights before. Reply to e-mail from your mother's coworker from the regional sales office's flirty cousin. Drain spaghetti and reserve a small cup of the cooking water.

Whisk together eggs and Parmesan and try to figure out what went wrong. You had boyfriends. Lots of them. Lord knows that if you're single for long enough the numbers add up. Some of them even seemed to like you. Maybe you've been too picky. It's not that you've been too focused on your career, because professionally speaking you're not that impressive. If the thought arises that the problem is that you are unlovable, push it down while gradually adding reserved pasta cooking water to egg mixture. Submit online profile to Match.com and hope you don't get a psychopath, or if he has to be a psychopath, that he has a respectable day job and can wear a suit well.

Return pasta to the skillet and pour egg mixture on top, stirring until eggs are no longer raw. Think of your own eggs, which are presumably hard boiled by now. Find name of sperm bank, just as a backup. Stir in bacon and parsley and enjoy with your cat.

YOU ARE OVERQUALIFIED FOR YOUR JOB AND THEY MAKE YOU GET THE DONUTS SUPER VEGGIE DOG

You will need:

Veggie dogs
Buns
Mustard
Ketchup
Relish
French-fried onions

Eat Your Feelings

Place Band-Aids on fingers to prevent mustard from getting in all the paper cuts you received while stuffing envelopes at work. In back of closet, find diploma from Harvard Business School. Decide to place it in a prominent place in your cubicle to let all the assistants know just who it is they are sending on errands. If you did not attend Harvard Business School, or any other school of recognizable worth, purchase banners, school posters, or athletic memorabilia from Harvard to create the appearance that you did.

Prepare veggie dogs according to package directions. In a small bowl, mix together mustard, ketchup, and relish. You should be able to calculate ⅓ of each condiment using skills learned when you acquired each of your several financial licenses (six, to be exact). None of which has thus far proved entirely necessary.

Spread condiment mixture on hot dog bun, place hot dog snugly inside, and top with french-fried onions. Eat hot dog as you run to pick up the dry cleaning for your firm's IT guy. Be sure to keep receipts for reimbursement on the off chance that you actually get reimbursed this time.

OT EVEN A TOTAL LOSER WOULD SLEEP WITH YOU OATMEAL COOKIES

You will need:

3 cups brown sugar
3 cups butter
6 cups oatmeal
1 Tbs. baking soda
3 cups flour
Lower standards

What went wrong this time? Sexy outfit? Check. Big beautiful hair? Check. Glimmering, pouting lips? Check. So how come you're home at 9:30 with the wrappers still on the condoms? Perhaps, as you suspected at the time, he really was autistic. Preheat the oven to 350°F.

Toss all ingredients in a large bowl. Use your hands to mix everything together. The dough will be dry—not quite as dry as your girl parts, but almost. Do a little math to figure out how many dates you have been on that ended with no happy ending. Answer: all of them. You thought this one would be good to go for sure—he had all the signs of someone desperate for action, right down to the lack of employment, severe stutter, and can of Axe sticking suggestively out of his backpack.

Form the dough into small balls—hey! Maybe the guy had really small balls and was just embarrassed to let you cradle them! Maybe you should call him and tell him that if that is the case you really don't mind—small is better than nothing, right? Maybe he will appreciate your candor. Or maybe he will take offense and tell you that his balls are huge, in which case you could simply respond, "Prove it." Butter the bottom of a glass or other flat object and coat with sugar; then smash the cookie balls flat onto an ungreased cookie sheet. (Ouch.) Bake for 10 minutes and lower standards to somewhere between grizzled recluse and registered sex offender.

A DHD ALPHABET SOUP

You will need:

8 oz. vegetable broth
Handful green beans, chopped
¼ cup kidney beans
¼ cup chopped carrots
1 can alphabet soup

Eat Your Feelings

Begin by pouring vegetable broth into a small soup pot. Lose interest in soup and decide to do the crossword puzzle instead. Fill in about half of puzzle. Stop. Remove all contents of refrigerator, deciding it needs cleaning. Decide this is quite dull and go to gym. When you get back from gym, put most of refrigerator contents back into fridge. Notice green beans, and remember soup. Chop beans into bite-sized pieces. Take a shower. Next, play solitaire on computer for 30–45 minutes as desired.

Back in the kitchen, restock rest of refrigerator. Chop carrots. Remember that you were supposed to call your mother because it was her birthday last week. Call your mom. When she answers, say, "Hi! Who's this?" to jog your memory of who it was you called. Let your mom do the talking so you don't really have to listen. While she rambles, sort out your CD collection. Place all CDs from college in one pile and sort the rest by genre. Then put all CDs in rack in no particular order.

The soup! Tell your mom you have to go. Sit in a chair and think of all the millions of things you need to do. Turn on television and watch *Golden Girls* marathon on Lifetime. When you notice that you are hungry—*stay with me now!*—go to kitchen. In cupboard—*eyes on me!*—find can of alphabet soup. *You still here? Good.* Open can of soup and put contents into a bowl. *Almost done, keep focus!* Heat bowl of soup in microwave and eat. *You did it!*

FOUND OUT YOUR BIRTH MOTHER WAS A CARNEY HOT BEEF SUNDAE

You will need:

½ lb. roast beef
1 package beef gravy mix
1 cup mashed potatoes
Handful shredded cheese
1 cherry tomato
Epsom salts

Warm roast beef in microwave for 30 seconds. Place in a bowl. Check teeth to make sure they are not falling out prematurely. Top roast beef with mashed potatoes. Call adoptive mother and demand more information: Did she run the dunk tank? Was she the cotton candy lady? Was she in the freak show—oh God, *was she in the freak show?*

Prepare gravy according to package directions. Have sudden horrifying thought: Who's the father? Rub temples, trying hard to suppress image of dirty toothless gimp that ran the Tilt-a-Whirl at the local fair and unexpectedly licked you that time. Pour desired amount of gravy on top of mashed potatoes and top with grated cheese.

Begin to understand your ability to contort your body into pretzel-like shapes, and put two and two together about the facial hair that's recently sprouted on your otherwise feminine jawline. Top beef sundae with cherry tomato and enjoy before soaking your webbed feet in hot bath of Epsom salts.

SALMON RUSHDIE FATWA SURPRISE

You will need:

2 salmon fillets
½ package puff pastry
3 Tbs. shallots, minced
Safe house
3 Tbs. chopped tarragon
2 tsp. chopped dill
1 egg, beaten
Kevlar vest
¼ cup white wine
¼ cup white wine vinegar
½ stick cold butter, cut into chunks

You will find this recipe is particularly useful if you are the author Salman Rushdie.

Make quick sweep of safe house to ensure that you are alone with your subversive writings. Preheat oven to 425°F. Roll out puff pastry on a floured surface and cut into two 12 × 6 inch squares. Use a sharp knife to make clean edges, keeping a firm grip on the handle to prevent it from being violently wrenched away from you by a sneaky terrorist. Put on Kevlar vest, just to be on the safe side.

Place 1 salmon fillet in center of each pastry square and season with salt and pepper. Top each with 1 Tbs. shallot, 1 Tbs. tarragon, and 1 tsp. dill. Use egg to brush edges of pastry. Fold long side then short side of pastry over salmon, forming a tidy little package. Seal edges.

Use excess puff pastry to create image of supreme leader of Iran. Give him large, pendulous breasts. Take photo of big-boobied ayatollah to post anonymously online. That'll show him.

Pop into oven and bake until brown, about 20 minutes or just long enough to begin follow-up novel *The Jihadist Wore Red*, the one about a lonely warrior for the glory of Islam who secretly yearns to be a rich and famous singer in a Vegas nightclub.

Boil wine, vinegar, and remainder of shallots in a small saucepan until reduced by half. Remove from heat and add butter one chunk at a time while repeating the phrase, "There is no God, there is no God, there is no God, but if there is a God let him like my books." Whisk in remainder of tarragon and pinch of salt and pepper. Cut salmon surprise into halves and serve with sauce.

Hide.

**E LIKES YOUR ROOMMATE
KEY LIME PIE**

You will need:

1 14 oz. can sweetened condensed milk
4 egg yolks
1 cup key lime juice
2 cups heavy cream
½ cup sugar
1 cup powdered weight gainer
1 9-inch graham cracker crust

Eat Your Feelings

Beat 2 egg yolks in a large bowl. Add condensed milk while remembering the first time the love of your life came over and spent the entire time talking to your roommate. Recall that your roommate seems to always be stepping out of the shower when he comes over. Add 2 more egg yolks to bowl and beat.

Preheat oven to 350°F. Ask yourself why it is that he and your roommate carry on their conversations in French when neither of them is from France. The only language skill you have is the quickly fading Old Prussian your grandfather insisted you learn. Add key lime juice to bowl.

In roommate's closet, check the sizes of her clothes. Try some of them on to see how you look. When you realize that you can't pull her skirts over your thighs, add 1 cup weight gainer protein powder to bowl and beat vigorously. Pour into pie shell and bake for 20 minutes or until set.

Chill pie and beat whipping cream together with sugar and slather all over pie. Being careful not to eat pie, or allow pie to touch skin in any way, leave pie in fridge with a note for roommate saying, "Made this just for you because you're the best roomie ever!" Sit back and watch her pack on the pounds.

CCIDENTALLY JOINED THE PTA PERFECT POTLUCK BAKED ZITI

You will need:

1 lb. ziti
1 pint ricotta cheese
1 jar pasta sauce
Booze
Garlic
¼ cup chopped parsley
1 cup shredded mozzarella
½ cup Parmesan cheese
Olive oil

Eat Your Feelings

You thought you would just "be a good parent." You thought, perhaps, it sounded like fun. Or maybe you were just bleary-eyed and hungover when you dropped your kid off and the teacher caught you off guard by saying, "I need someone to be on the PTA," and you just said, "Yeah, sure." Whatever the case, you could never have imagined the bureaucratic nightmare that is the PTA. And now, at least once a semester, you will be asked to provide something for a potluck dinner, a potluck dinner you have no desire to attend. Here is what you do:

Preheat oven to 400°F. Cook pasta according to package directions. Send e-mail to PTA president, lobbying strongly for the inclusion of alcoholic beverages in all potluck evenings. Mix sauce with pasta, stirring to coat. Butter bottom of a lasagna dish. Spread a layer of pasta on the bottom of the dish. Beg spouse to come with you to PTA meetings. Or better yet, to go in your place. When he says no, threaten divorce and call him a bad father. But not in front of the kids. Save the big guns for later.

Mix all three cheeses together with parsley, reserving some Parmesan to sprinkle on top.

Mix ricotta in with pasta. Now is the time to start drinking—not heavily, just enough to numb yourself against the tedium of forty-seven parents complaining about nonorganic snacks and the heaviness of backpacks for three hours.

Layer remaining pasta in dish and cover with additional sauce. Top with Parmesan cheese and a drizzle of olive oil. Bake for 10–15 minutes or until bubbly, enjoying a bit more liquor, but not enough that you will smell like booze. If you do smell like booze, rub some garlic over your skin to cover the scent (and to make it seem as though your ziti is authentic).

Approach spouse once again, telling him that you feel like you're getting sick, that you just threw up, whatever it takes. When he still won't agree to go in your place, tell the children that their teacher was supposed to see Daddy at the school tonight, but Daddy's thinking of not going. Run from room.

When even this tactic fails, resign yourself to attending the potluck, telling yourself that maybe the PTA *needs* you. Maybe they would be lost without you. Decide to nominate yourself for PTA president and phone prominent elderly politician to inquire if he is looking for a spunky young running mate.

OUBLE-DETOX MILK SHAKE

You will need:

1 pint ice cream
1 8 oz. container hot fudge sauce

It is imperative when making this recipe to keep the blinds or curtains shut to avoid excess sunlight and to keep the neighbors from seeing for themselves just what a horrid lush you have become.

Using very slow, controlled movements so as not to induce vomiting, remove container of ice cream from the freezer. Do not use more than 1 pint of ice cream or vomiting will surely ensue (unless of course your ice cream of choice is Baskin-Robbins Mint Chocolate Chip, which may be eaten in limitless quantities). Place container in microwave, set on high, for 25 seconds or until soft enough to drink. Drink ½ of milk-shakeish concoction directly from carton. Very important: Do not try to find a glass—they are all lined with the syrupy, goopy residue of tequila, Southern Comfort, or whatever strange beverage that guy from Newark was drinking last night and will inspire vomiting.

Empty contents of fudge sauce into ice cream container and slosh around. Do not use spoons because Newark guy's junkie friend was over, too, and the spoons were most likely used to "cook up" narcotics. The last thing you need is a serious drug addiction on top of your alcohol dependency. Place ice cream container back in microwave, set on high, for 20 seconds. Swish container around again and drink. Do not attempt to lie down upon finishing shake, as that may result in vomiting. Just stand very still until movement can commence in a steady fashion.

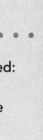OME FRIES FOR THE UNINSURED

You will need:

Plastic knife
2 potatoes
Canola oil
½ onion
½ green pepper
Mrs. Dash
Salt
Pepper
Q-Tip
Bourbon
Flashlight
Mirror

Peel and thinly slice potatoes using plastic knife, as you are unable to afford the financial burden of losing a digit or parts thereof. Cut onion and pepper into chunks. Wearing flame-retardant clothing, as skin grafts are extremely costly, pour enough oil to coat a skillet and warm over medium-high heat.

Layer potatoes in the pan, topping with onions and peppers. Sprinkle with salt, pepper, and Mrs. Dash. Cover and let cook for 10 minutes or until potatoes are brown on the bottom. Add more oil to the pan and flip potatoes—very carefully—to brown the other side.

Call a friend and offer her fifty dollars to come over and give you a Pap smear. When she reminds you that she is not a doctor, tell her to stop nitpicking and assure her that you will provide the Q-Tips. Cook potatoes for 10 minutes more, until brown and crisp. Enjoy with bourbon to loosen you up, and then using flashlight and mirror perform auto-colonoscopy. Wash hands.

LEPT WITH YOUR PROFESSOR AND HE STILL GAVE YOU A D BAKED BRIE

You will need:

1 round loaf crusty bread
1 small wheel brie
Dried cherries

Let's begin by recognizing that your paper on Jacobean tragedy and its parallels with the Reagan administration was deserving of at least a B. The connection between Jerry Falwell and Ferdinand in John Webster's *The Duchess of Malfi* was inspired. Preheat oven to 350°F.

Call academic adviser and discuss possibility of taking the class pass/fail so as not to ruin your hard-earned GPA. Slice off top of bread, cut into triangles, and reserve. Scoop out a well in bread the size of cheese. Consider changing majors. Visualize the math department staff naked and abandon idea. Place brie inside bread.

Slowly allow the thought to enter your mind that the lousy grade was reflective not of your paper, but of your performance last Thursday evening in the faculty lounge. Perhaps the spanking was not appreciated. Is it possible that your tears were misinterpreted?

Place bread on a baking sheet and place in oven on middle rack. Remember how he buried his face in the middle of your rack. Bake until cheese is as bubbling and melted as your heart when he read from his book of self-published poetry. Enjoy brie with bread triangles while writing first chapter of a scandalous tell-all novel that will end your professor's career and make tiresome GPA maintenance totally inconsequential.

UNWANTED PREGNANCY
KIELBASA AND SAUERKRAUT

You will need:

$9.49
Kielbasa, sliced into 6 pieces
1 jar sauerkraut
2 potatoes
Ketchup
Caraway seeds
2 apples
1 onion
2 Tbs. brown sugar

Count out $9.49 from change jar. Go to drugstore and buy generic brand pregnancy test. After you slide your pile of change across the counter, resist slapping the cashier when he says, "Good luck, Mommy."

At home, take test. When it is confirmed that you are pregnant, try to determine who the hell did this to you. If you can pinpoint the guilty party, it is a good idea to tell him, provided that you know his name and phone number. The subsequent conversation can range in tone from unpleasant to extremely unpleasant.

Open jar of sauerkraut and rinse under cold water. Peel and chop apples and potatoes and place into a large pot with kielbasa, sauerkraut, chopped onion, and a good squeeze of ketchup. Sprinkle on caraway seeds, top with lid, and let simmer while you make some hard decisions. If you are considering putting unwanted baby up for adoption, make a list of qualities you would look for in an adoptive family for your mistake. Included in that list should be:

> Must have home
> Must have job or other means to support child that does not include
>   a crystal-meth lab
> Must not be crazy people
> Must not be likely to sell child on black market (as far as you know)
> Must not have room in attic or basement where thirty adopted
>   children work sewing soccer balls or making Hello Kitty pencil
>   cases
> Family pet—good
> Family dog-fighting ring—bad

Eat Your Feelings

Sit for a while and feel sorry for your pregnant self, knowing full well that it is your fault. Except in cases where it is not at all your fault. Sprinkle brown sugar into pot, and let simmer until potatoes are fully cooked. Eat while considering all options, being mindful that you are eating for two. Sorry.

HREE-ALARM CHILI FOR BAD MOTHERS

You will need:

1 lb. ground beef
Soundproofing
2 Tbs. oil
1 large onion, chopped
2 cloves garlic, minced
1 28 oz. can tomatoes
2 tsp. chili powder
1 Tbs. brown sugar
Pinch oregano
Salt
Hefty pinch crushed red pepper
1 can kidney beans, drained
1 red pepper, diced
Xanax

Install soundproofing to prevent neighbors from calling child-protection services when they hear you screaming at your children. Brown beef in a pan with onions, garlic, and pepper. Put toddler to bed. When she refuses to stay quietly in her room, take away Mr. Snuggles, her bear. If she still refuses to be quiet, tell her that you gave Mr. Snuggles to a little girl named Stacy, who knows how to be quiet at bedtime. If this still does not work, tell her that you have arranged for her to sleep at the neighbor's house and have her put on her shoes.

Drain fat from pan and add tomatoes, sugar, chili powder and oregano. Call in ten-year-old son to help you. When he accidentally spills some tomato on the counter, scream, "That's it, you clumsy reject. I'm outta here!" Then tell him that you have no idea who his real father is. Bring all ingredients to a boil and reduce heat to simmer for 1 hour. Grab your keys and go out for a beer.

Steal seventeen-year-old son's cell phone and text all his super-hot friends to come over. Put on your tightest, shortest skirt and a push-up bra. Smear on some black eyeliner to distract from the bags. Add beans to pot and simmer for 15 minutes more. Enjoy chili with son's friends, taking care to spill some on your heaving breasts and suggestively lick it off with your tongue.

TWENTY-NINE AND STILL CAN'T PAY YOUR RENT VEGGIE SANDWICH

You will need:

Recycling center
Absence of pride
Internet access
Bun

Take one month's worth of empty beer cans to recycling center. Stand in line and when it is your turn feed your cans into the machine and collect money. Do not be tempted to buy gum ball from a machine for twenty-five cents—that's five cans! Instead head to a friend's house (make sure they have Internet access) and post an ad on craigslist, offering whatever services you can. If you have no available services, consider offering your back as advertising space, donating body fluids, or medical testing.

Head to nearest Roy Rogers and purchase a single, plain bun. Stop off at the free Fixin's Bar and load that sucker up with all the lettuce, tomato, onion, and pickles you can handle. Smother in your choice of condiment.

Call parents and beg for assistance with rent. Use as incentive the threat to donate eggs or sperm, painting vivid portrait of their potential grandchildren on sale to the general public.

You will need:

Maize
Squash
Pelts
Pumpkin
Wampum
Pheasants

Eat Your Feelings

Grind maize with stones to make a grain. Add to this grain the sweet substance of the bee, salt, and water. Make into a pancake and cook over fire. You will be able to bring to palefaces who are camped near the shoreline. You hear the white men will offer three axe handles and much wampum for the Great Brother Mountain and cannot believe they would be so wrong-minded—who could own a mountain? You will gladly take the axe handles, for this winter will be harsh and much wood will be needed.

Bring maize cake to camp. As you approach, put your hand up to show that you come in peace. Run fast when they take out their fire sticks and point their lightning at you. They must not have need for maize cakes.

Decide that the white men need some pelts to keep them warm in the long winter that is ahead. This time, bring pelts and also squash, beans, and several pheasants, to show good will. As you approach, put your hand up and show them the pelts. When their womenfolk begin to scream, take this as a sign that they are going to get their fire sticks. Run swiftly as a deer into the cover of the forest.

Seek help of your great chief, Massasoit, who took you in when the white folk tried to enslave you and then killed all your tribe. Massasoit counsels you to return again, because these poor confused people will have no hope of surviving the winter if you don't help them with food and pelts. Massasoit advises to bring a pumpkin—among men is there one who does not like pumpkins? And his word is wise. Also bring wampum and beads for the women.

Try to avoid giving the food to the white men with the funny shoes with buckles on them—they are skittish and quick to anger. If necessary, sneak into camp at night and just leave the food and pelts for them. Do not accept, in trade for food and pelts, any blankets from the white man! These blankets are covered with the germs of smallpox and will send you to the spirit world.

One day these people will honor you for saving their lives, with the painting of a warrior chief. It will be on a hat that is worn in a game played with the skin of a pig. And you will have great justice when fat white folk in skins called "tracksuits" give you much wampum in large wigwams called "casinos."

YOU STOPPED SLEEPING WITH YOUR HUSBAND YEARS AGO PROVENÇAL TOMATO TARTLET

You will need:

1 package puff pastry, defrosted
Olive oil
1 can plum tomatoes, whole
1 clove garlic, crushed
1 onion, thinly sliced
Small knob of butter
1 cup Gruyère, shredded
Sliced olives
1 Tbs. herbes de Provence

Preheat oven to 325°F. Wearing the velour tracksuit that has become your uniform, roll out puff pastry on a parchment-lined baking sheet and brush with olive oil. When husband enters room, try to hide disdain. Quickly move when he comes near you so as not to make actual bodily contact—don't want to give him the wrong idea! Place tomatoes in a sauce pot and set on stove over medium heat. Add herbs and garlic.

Using time you have saved by giving up painful personal-grooming appointments, slice onions very thin and sauté in butter over low heat until caramelized.

Score the edge of the pastry, being careful not to push the knife all the way through the dough. Suspiciously eye husband to see if he is attractively dressed or smelling nicely or smiling for no reason. When it is certain that he is still the annoying, depressing guy he was when he left the house that morning, relax in the knowledge that he is not looking for sex outside the marriage. Or even if he is looking for it, that potbelly tells you he's not getting it. Just because you're not sleeping with him doesn't mean you want him sleeping with anyone else.

If husband looks at you in suggestive manner, employ one of the following techniques:

1. Pass gas
2. Talk about your yeast infection
3. Ask if he has called his mother lately
4. Casually ask if he has seen the maxi pads
5. Play your Indigo Girls collection and excitedly sing along, using hairbrush as microphone

Spread tomatoes on pastry and top with onions. Cover with shredded Gruyère and scatter olives over the top. While tart bakes, for 20–25 minutes or until pastry is golden brown and cheese is bubbling, pretend not to notice as husband takes unusually long time in the bathroom.

RAINBOW SHERBET 'CAUSE YOUR BOSS IS A PERVERT

You will need:

Small tape recorder
One wafer cone
One scoop rainbow sherbet
Attorney
New job

Eat Your Feelings

At work, act as though everything is normal. When your boss shouts out, "Hey! Who did you go home with last night—you're walking a little bow-legged!" just ignore him. When he stands near your cubicle, sniffs the air, and says, "Smells like somebody's in heat!" just keep your head down and say nothing. When he calls you into his office to show you photos of a woman in an acrobatic position with a horse, just say, "Oh, look at that." Then leave.

Quietly enter all of these instances into your journal. Turn on small tape recorder in your pocket and ask him if he likes your new shoes, so that you can record his response: "I'd like 'em better if your feet were up around your ears." Tell your boss you have a dentist appointment.

Take tape and journal to attorney. Stop by ice cream parlor of choice and ask for an extra-large cone of rainbow sherbet. Return to office in time for process server to hand your boss the papers. When the papers have been handed over, shove cone in your boss's face. Those added calories won't help in your upcoming job search.

EVIL STEPMOTHER'S ROCK CANDY

You will need:

- Sugar
- Food coloring
- String
- Wax paper
- Galvanized washers
- Ajax
- Ipecac

Eat Your Feelings

Tell your stepchildren that you are going to make them rock candy. Be sure their father is around when you make the announcement so that he sees how wonderful you are with his children. Invent a story about how the making of rock candy was a tradition in your family and you want to share it with them—your *new* family. Ignore blank stares and scornful scoffs.

In kitchen, tell children to gather around the stove. When they reluctantly comply, boil 2 cups water and add sugar, stirring until dissolved. Pour boiling hot sugar mixture into as many jars as you have spoiled, selfish stepchildren. Do not "accidentally" spill insanely hot liquid on the children, as that would result in their father feeling sorry for them. That's sympathy *you're* entitled to.

Ask them what color they would like their candy to be. Place each kid's desired coloring into its respective jar. Tie one end of string to washer to act as a weight. Dip string into jar and then lay it flat on a piece of wax paper for a few days. Children will inevitably lose interest in the project. At this time, discard the lot and purchase rock candy from a store. For a particularly rotten stepchild, spray rock candy with cleanser containing bleach. If you go this route, be sure to have vomit-inducing ipecac on hand. No need to go to prison over these brats.

P MS POT STICKERS

You will need:

40 wonton wrappers
½ pound ground pork
1 egg
Chocolate
¼ cup chopped scallion
¼ cup shredded carrots
¼ cup duck sauce
Water
1½ cups oil for frying
Midol
Someone to yell at
½ cup soy sauce
1 tsp. sesame oil

Remove medieval torture device otherwise known as a bra. Put on comfy sweat pants to allow for bloating. If someone should cross your path as you go to change, yell at them. If they cross your path again, give them a good shove so they don't do it again.

Preheat oven to 200°F. In a large bowl, combine pork, egg, scallion, carrots, and duck sauce. Eat chocolate. Place one wonton in front of you and brush sides with water. Place ½ tsp. pork mixture in center of wonton. Do not mindlessly eat pork mixture or confuse it with chocolate, as raw pork is teeming with deadly bacteria and will kill you. Fold wonton and seal edges. Place wonton on a baking sheet under a damp towel. Repeat with remaining wontons.

Place a large nonstick skillet over high heat and add 1 Tbs. oil, to coat bottom. Take Midol to combat both cramps and the splitting headache that has resulted from the filling and folding of so many wontons. Rethink decision to embark on such a tedious endeavor. After all, pot stickers are just a phone call away. Consider the limp greasy mess that is a delivery order of pot stickers and place 10 dumplings in the hot pan and fry for 2 minutes until the bottoms are golden brown. Add 1 cup water and cover, cooking 5 minutes or until water is absorbed. Place on baking sheet in warmed oven and repeat with remaining wontons.

Mix soy sauce and sesame oil together. Dunk pot stickers into dipping sauce while having a good cry and trying to remember that PMS is far better than the alternatives: pregnancy, menopause, or a complete hysterectomy.

DUMPED ON NEW YEAR'S EVE MEATBALL SANDWICH

You will need:

1 loaf Italian bread
Butter
1 cup tomato sauce
10 frozen meatballs
½ cup shredded mozzarella
Parmesan cheese
Large box

Eat Your Feelings

Take off party dress—you aren't going anywhere. Throw party hats and noisemakers in garbage. Close windows and turn on music very loud so as not to hear revelers in the street. But don't discard the champagne— that would be a terrible idea. In fact, pour yourself a large tumbler of it and preheat the oven to 325°F.

Slice bread lengthwise just as your former boyfriend sliced through your heart. Spread butter on both sides of bread and place in the oven until lightly toasted. Prepare meatballs according to package directions. Stop crying before handling hot meatballs. Take five deep breaths to calm heaving sobs. Remove bread from oven and place on a baking sheet.

Arrange meatballs on bread and top with sauce and mozzarella, reserving two meatballs and a little bit of sauce. Take stupid snow globe that your ex-boyfriend thought was a romantic Christmas gift and throw it out the window just to hear it smash on the street. If it should hit a New Year's Eve reveler on the head, all the better. In any case, they will most likely be too drunk to remember it.

Sprinkle Parmesan cheese over sandwich and return to oven. Squeeze together reserved meatballs and sauce to resemble fecal matter. Place in box. Plaster with ex-boyfriend's address and place by door so you don't forget to take it to post office when it opens on January 2. Bake sandwich until cheese is melted and enjoy with more champagne as you consider that things could be worse—you could be Dick Clark.

UGLY BABY CHEESE SANDWICH

You will need:

2 slices white bread
1 pack sliced Monterey Jack cheese
1 firm, ripe tomato
CGI software
1 pack of chips

Toast bread until lightly brown. Place 3–4 slices of cheese on 1 piece of toasted bread. Cut 1 thick slice of the tomato and lay on top of cheese. Do not lay a picture of Shiloh Jolie-Pitt over your baby's face, because although this will improve the aesthetics of the infant, it may cause suffocation or further disfigurement via paper cuts.

Using CGI software, create images of how baby will look in ten, twenty, thirty years. It is best to brace for the worst, as ugly toddlers and teens can be even worse than ugly babies. Keep in mind—Bill Gates probably did not win any cutest-baby contests.

Carefully take a handful of chips and place them on top of the tomato. Reinvest your baby's college-fund money in plastic-surgery savings account and set aside extra money to purchase future prom dates. Gently press other slice of toasted bread on top. Microwave for approximately 25 seconds or until cheese has fully melted. Serve sandwich with side of chips and tell others your real baby was switched at birth.

MIDLIFE CRISIS RIB EYE

You will need:

Ferrari
1 large rib-eye steak
Butter
Salt
Pepper
Young girlfriend

Eat Your Feelings

Wake to find gray hair where you previously had none. In a panic manifested by an overwhelming sense of looming mortality, divorce wife. Rent snazzy apartment in midtown high-rise and furnish it entirely in beige leather and hang portraits of famous boxers on the walls. At nearby butcher, buy meatiest, grizzliest piece of rib eye available.

Once home, smear steak with butter, season with salt and pepper, and turn the grill on high, just like your blood pressure is going to be when this is all over. Call young lady friend (a former babysitter or daughter of a friend will do). She must be fifteen to twenty years younger than you, any more and it's just gross.

Place rib eye on grill and call Ferrari dealer. No need to take a test-drive: You've been dreaming about this car since you were eighteen, and you *deserve* it! Have them send over a Gran Turismo, in cherry red, with a white leather interior and a really loud sound system to blast your girl-friend's Avril Lavigne CDs. It would also be a good idea to make it a convertible so that you can spend the summer driving around showing off the bulging muscles you plan to get after all those hours you plan on spending in the gym.

After 3 minutes, flip steak, and return call from your children's psychiatrist. Make appointment for tedious family therapy session. It's going to be a drag, so be sure to line up fun evening with girlfriend for later in the night—perhaps dancing?

When steak is done, dig in with no fear of clogging your aging, tired arteries. So what if the clock is ticking? You only live once.

SINGLE MOTHER BEEF STEW

You will need:

4 8 oz. cans diet Red Bull
1 lb. stew beef
2 stalks celery, chopped
2 carrots, chopped
Babysitter
½ lb. new potatoes
1 onion
2 cups red wine
1 bay leaf
Salt and pepper
8 hours

Eat Your Feelings

Open 8 oz. can Red Bull. Cut stew beef into chunks. Wake sixteen-year-old Trevor. This can only be accomplished through screaming and threats to take away cell phone and Wii. Hide Trevor's reptilian contact lenses and encourage him not to wear so much white pancake makeup for one day.

Check on twelve-year-old Lisa, who has been up since 5:30 a.m. straightening her hair. Make her remove excessive eyeliner. Sign note from her teacher telling her you are aware of her plummeting math grades.

Time to wake one-year-old Oscar. Give in to urge to crawl into crib for a quick snuggle. Fall asleep and have brief dream about being twenty-two and having sex with your college boyfriend. Wake in a cold sweat when Oscar sticks finger up your nose.

Throw freezer waffles into family-size toaster to take care of breakfast. Open one more Red Bull. Drink.

Peel and chop carrots. Place all ingredients in a Crock-Pot set to "slow cook" while waiting for babysitter to arrive. As horrid realization that the sitter isn't going to show sets in, open another Red Bull, resisting urge to add vodka. Breathe deeply as you call every disgruntled former babysitter and offer them exorbitant amounts of money, all to no avail.

Put older kids on school bus and bring baby to work. Smuggle baby into office in backpack. Place him under your desk with toys. The following office supplies make suitable toys: tape, Post-its, nonlead pencils. The following do not make suitable toys: X-Acto knives, letter openers, staplers, ink cartridges, box cutters, the mailroom guy.

Have one medium-size workplace tantrum. It is important to let everyone know just how hard life is for you at the moment: It will elicit sympathy or, at the very least, keep people from bothering you with more work. It may also help drown out the noise of the baby.

After work, take baby to Lisa's soccer game. Embarrass Lisa with your excessive cheering as you try and avoid idle chitchat with other "happily" married mothers who only want to set you up with their fathers.

At home, the stew should be done. Remove bay leaf. Call down to basement to tell Trevor dinner is ready and that his friend Toby can stay. Doesn't Toby have his *own* home? Serve over rice or noodles.

EAD BROKE DUMPLINGS

You will need:

½ package noodles, any variety
Cabbage
Carrots
6 packs soy sauce
Handful of bean sprouts

Perhaps you majored in art history and have unable to fine a suitable position as an art historian. Perhaps your custom-ribbon watch company went belly up. Perhaps corporations have not been as eager to advertise on your blog as you had anticipated. Or perhaps you are just lazy and unmotivated. Whatever the case, if you are dead broke this one is for you! While not traditional dumplings, you will find that if you close your eyes and think of dumplings while you are eating, the taste will be the same.

Boil noodles according to package directions. This may be done on a traditional stove or over an open fire, hobo style, if things are that bad. Slice cabbage into thin strips. If no knife is available, just rip it up.

Julienne carrots into matchsticks. Again this may be accomplished with a sharp knife, a bumpy rock, or by nibbling the carrots into the desired shape.

Sauté cabbage and carrots in soy sauce packs taken from sushi bar or Japanese restaurant, about 2 minutes or until soft. Add sprouts and noodles along with additional soy sauce to taste.

Eat while thinking of Asian things.

$\mathcal{H}$E'S BETTER OFF WITHOUT YOU LINGUINI WITH SUN-DRIED TOMATO CREAM SAUCE

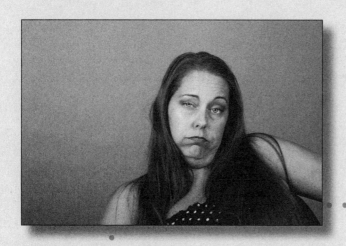

You will need:

1 lb. linguini
2 Tbs. butter
1 clove garlic
1 cup vegetable broth
½ cup sun-dried tomatoes, cut into quarters
1 cup heavy cream

Melt butter in a heavy saucepan over medium-high heat. Add garlic, broth, and tomatoes and bring to a boil. Simmer for 10 minutes. In mirror, take a good long look at yourself. Note the puffy eyes, bloodshot from all the screaming and nagging you do. Note the clumps of hair you have torn out in frustration when he has not called you back *immediately*. And note your shabby, unfashionable clothes. It's really amazing that he ever went out with you at all.

Prepare pasta according to package directions. You should be good at following directions, because you sure expect people to follow yours. Remember the time that you ridiculed your ex in front of his whole family by barking at him for folding your clothes the wrong way? You look like a donkey when you're shouting. And like a warthog when you're not.

Add cream and bring to boil, simmering until cream is thick enough to coat the back of a spoon or as thick as your appalling Boston accent. Look at photos of ex-boyfriend. Note how handsome he is but how he looks so sad. See how you are clinging to him in every photo, grimacing and tight lipped?

Now look at recent photos: Facebook photos taken at his wedding to the wealthy Italian supermodel turned political activist. See how he's smiling? See how gorgeous she is? That can never be you. Never. Who were you kidding in the first place?

Pour sauce over pasta, top with Parmesan cheese, and wait for the next unsuspecting patsy to come along so you can project your self-hatred onto him.

YOUR DREAMS WILL NEVER COME TRUE HUNGARIAN GOULASH

You will need:

2½ lb. stew beef

2 Tbs. butter

2 onions, chopped

2 Tbs. paprika

2 cups white wine

2 bay leaves

4 large potatoes, peeled and chopped

Backup plan

TWO WEEKS IN ADVANCE

Send out cards announcing your farewell performance. Be sure to invite everyone you have ever worked with, either in your failed attempt at a career in musical theater or in the many restaurants, retail, and temporary work situations that have sustained you these past years. Also invite the neighbors and the elderly in the likely event that none of the aforementioned people show up.

Put together a top-quality cabaret show. Include the songs you sing best, a few comedic pieces, and at least one dramatic monologue set to cello and French horn. Then begin to save your money because your MFA is now exactly that, a master of fuck all, and you will need additional education if you want to begin a career that does not require you to be able to dance (tap, jazz) and do accents (American southern, American mid-Atlantic, standard British, French).

THE DAY OF

Melt butter in a large pot over medium heat. Add chopped onions and sauté for 7 minutes until they begin to brown. Add chopped beef, turning to brown all sides. Pour in wine, add bay leaves and chopped potatoes, and simmer for 2 hours.

As guests arrive be sure to charge admission—the money will come in handy!

Eat Your Feelings

While performing try to keep the emotions to an appropriate level. Remember that if people really cared about your theatrical endeavors, you wouldn't be a fifty-year-old cater waiter.

When audience leaves, after the third encore, enjoy goulash over egg noodles with a dollop of sour cream and a bucket of pity, while attempting to pick yourself out of the crowd of blurry extras from that one time you were in a real Hollywood movie.

# YOU DID NOT SIGN UP FOR THIS CRAP CRÊPES SUZETTE FOR WIVES OF FORMER BANKERS

You will need:

eBay
3 eggs
2 Tbs. flour
Someone who doesn't mind your whining
1 Tbs. water
1 Tbs. milk
Pinch of salt
A job

Who does he think he is? He has a *responsibility* to make the kind of money you married him for. It is his *duty*—otherwise you could sue him for misrepresenting his earning potential. If you *wanted* to work for a living, you would have married someone cute, or at least interesting. Crack three eggs over his head. On second thought, crack them into a bowl, and make yourself some crêpes suzette like you used to enjoy for brunch (when you could afford brunch).

All the lovely little dresses you bought last season in Paris, before every-thing went to hell, are on eBay for just *anyone* to bid on. The thought of some girl in Des Moines wearing your vintage Halston understandably makes you want to puke. Hope someone buys that stuff soon, because you need to buy comfortable shoes—it sure is hard to wait tables in heels! Put flour into eggs with the water and milk and a pinch of salt to represent the tears you shed for yourself.

All he does is lie around and mope all day. His friends tell you that you need to look out for him, that his depression is bordering on dangerous. Well, excuse you. How is that *your* fault? You didn't sign up to be in-volved with some poor, lazy, depressed guy in an entry-level position at freaking IBM. Ugh! Just listen to him crying! Pathetic.

Pour a bit of batter into a buttery hot pan, and cook your thin crêpes one at a time. That's better. When a girl can't count on her rich husband to be rich, at least she can count on some crêpes. When they are done sprinkle them with sugar and kirsch. Oh . . . no kirsch. Too *expensive*. THIS IS JUST TOO MUCH. What kind of a life are you supposed to have if you can't buy kirsch? There he is, crying again. It's so embarrassing for you. You did not buy a ticket to this show. This show sucks.

Y OUR DAD IS A SCUMBAG MONKEY BREAD

You will need:

1 cup white sugar
1 cup brown sugar
1 Tbs. cinnamon
½ cup of butter
1 tsp. vanilla
Butterscotch pudding powder
3 tubes of refrigerated dinner roll dough

Eat Your Feelings

Preheat oven to 350°F. Mix together cinnamon and white sugar in a large ziplock bag. Be sure the bag is clean and hasn't been used by your father to transport narcotics or other paraphernalia home from clubs. Grease the bottom of a Bundt pan. The grease should be about as thick as the grease in your father's hair. Not his chest hair—that would be too greasy.

Open tubes of dinner rolls, suppressing memory of the last dinner you had with your father, when he started caressing the waitress's doughy buttock and you were thrown out of your favorite restaurant. Using a knife dipped in water, cut rolls into quarters. Put rolls into ziplock bag and shake, coating each ball like your father coats his with anti-itch medicated foot powder.

Layer the dough in the Bundt pan, sprinkling each layer with pudding powder as you go. In a saucepan, melt butter. Add brown sugar and boil for 1 minute. Remember the time your father had a huge boil on his neck and made a video of himself popping it and posted it on YouTube. Add vanilla. Pour over dough in pan.

Bake in oven for 30–40 minutes. To eat, pull apart dough balls with fingers. If sharing with father, make him wash his hands. You don't know where they've been.

HUMMUS FOR WHEN YOU WANT TO KILL SOMEONE

You will need:

1 can chickpeas
1 clove garlic
⅓ cup tahini
2 Tbs. olive oil
Lemon
Salt
Parsley
Pita

There are two ways to make this hummus. The first way is for when you just *feel* like you want to kill someone. For the second method, please see the following recipe.

Tear off the top of the can of chickpeas—you're so angry, this won't be difficult. Place chickpeas in a food processor, imagining each round bean is the head of your intended victim. Talk to the little heads, saying things like, "Get in there and keep quiet. Serves you right for snooping through my e-mails. Next time you'll think twice before telling the boss that my work is sloppy. We'll see who is sloppy *now*." Pulse the blade a few times, not to fully puree the beans, but just to make them suffer a little.

Add garlic, tahini, and boiling olive oil to bowl of processor, imagining the victim's screams as they are burned alive while you shout, "Why do you always send e-mails at 11:00 p.m. to make it look like you're still working? Who does that?" Quickly add lemon juice, squeezing hard to get all the juice in their lesions, yelling now, loudly, "This is for the ten thousand times a day I have to hear you quote lines from *Fletch* in your horrible nasally voice, which reverberates off my cubicle walls and chips away at my very soul." And then, the pièce de résistance: the salt. Scream, "I don't care if you *did* get promoted; you will never be the boss of me! Who's the boss *now*, pal?" Really get in there and rub the salt around in the wounds with your fingers if necessary, but watch out that you avoid the blade of the food processor 'cause it could cut your fingers off.

Now with a loud evil laugh, pulse the processor over and over until the hummus is a thick puree. Sprinkle with chopped parsley and enjoy with pita and deep breaths.

HUMMUS FOR WHEN YOU HAVE KILLED SOMEONE

You will need:

1 can chickpeas
1 clove garlic
Rubber gloves
⅓ cup tahini
2 Tbs. olive oil
Wood chipper
Squeeze of lemon
Large plastic tarp
Body-size container
Antibacterial cleanser with bleach

Check to make sure victim is actually dead. Once you are sure, absolutely sure, drag him outside. Set up a large tarp in a secluded area where you have placed wood chipper. This is the easy part. Simply feed him into chipper and catch resultant mulch in container. Once body is fully chipped, clean inside and out with cleanser.

Shower, being certain to clean off any blood and tissue that may have flown around in the chipping process. In kitchen, place all ingredients into a food processor—exactly the way you did with your victim. Whiz it up and pack into a container with pita. Enjoy hummus as you dump your human mulch into ocean.

FANNIE MAE AND FREDDIE MAC 'N' CHEESE

You will need:

2 packages government cheese or other cheese
2 boxes noodles: elbows, shells preferred
Pinch cayenne
1 ration powdered milk
1 Tbs. flour
1 Tbs. butter, or lard if butter is not available
Water

Eat Your Feelings

It has been months since the financial world imploded and your 401K is now "worth" negative $250,000. Now you're stuck with a giant house and no way of paying for it. Time to get resourceful. You're hungry, but, more important, the people who rent your guest rooms, the people who rent cot space in the upstairs hall, the family that lives in the finished basement, and the gang of ex hedge fund managers turned hoboes— well, they're hungry too. Someone's got to feed them.

Ride your bicycle to the supermarket in town. Never mind about your disheveled appearance, you're not going in. Instead forage in the dumpsters for packages of pasta and any fruits or vegetables you can find. Also keep a lookout for dented cans and moldy cheese. Cheese is essentially a mold-based food, in any case, so any green bits can easily be discarded.

On the way home, scan the side of the road for wild herbs. Often you can find onions and rosemary, which can be bundled and either used in cooking or sold to people who still have money, if there are any.

On the Viking range in your McMansion, mix powdered milk with water. Put butter and flour into a small pot, mixing constantly over medium heat (if you still have utilities) to make a roux. Add milk and let simmer.

Prepare pasta according to package directions. While pasta cooks, get to work on your chores:

> You need more cots.
> Place clean sheets on all beds in guest rooms and clean towels in the baths for the boarders that will be moving in this afternoon.
> Pick up laundry from bins outside rooms that have already been let.
> Start the ironing you have been taking in to help make ends meet.

Gather eggs from chicken coop. Check to make sure the "Eggs for Sale" sign at the end of the cul-de-sac is clearly visible.

Mix cheese with milk sauce until melted. Drain pasta and add to sauce, stirring to coat evenly. If you found any dented cans of peas, open the can and give it a good sniff. If it smells vaguely of botulism, throw it out! If not, add the peas to the macaroni and cheese.

Bash metal soup ladle against large iron triangle to let the hedge fund managers know that lunch is on the table. Spoon macaroni into small bowls to make it look more plentiful. Thank the tenants for doing odd jobs for you. Sprinkle a bit too much cayenne pepper on top of each bowl to ensure that they won't want seconds.

Dear Reader,

I have given you the tools to figure out what to eat, but there is so much more to learn! On the following pages you will find some helpful hints on the best environments for eating your feelings. No need to limit yourself just to the darkened kitchen when you're feeling downtrodden.

Warmest Regards,
Heather Whaley

Some places to eat your feelings:

Bathroom

The office

The White House

Hallways

Public toilets

Airplanes

A stairwell

Across the street from your ex-boyfriend's house

Across the street from where your ex-boyfriend works

Across the street from where your ex-boyfriend's new girlfriend lives

Under your ex-boyfriend's bed

Church

In midair while skydiving (not recommended)

Criminal courthouse

Halfway inside the refrigerator

The Laundromat

The DMV

Food court (preferred)

In your parked car

In a friend's parked car

The attic

In bed

Parole office

Window ledge

Floor of the stock exchange

Bus depot

The prom

Some books to read while eating your feelings:

War and Peace by Leo Tolstoy

The Catcher in the Rye by J. D. Salinger

You'll Never Eat Lunch in This Town Again by Julia Phillips

Helter Skelter by Vincent Bugliosi

People magazine

Don't Make Me Stop This Car: Adventures in Fatherhood by Al Roker

Flowers in the Attic by V. C. Andrews

Lolita by Vladimir Nabokov

Things I Overheard While Talking to Myself by Alan Alda

Are You There God? It's Me, Margaret by Judy Blume

User's Manual Guide to Troubleshooting iMac and iPhone

*Don't Let Your Kids Kill You: A Guide for Parents of Drug and Alcohol Addicted
    Children* by Charles Rubin

Alcoholics Anonymous Big Book by AA Services

Twilight by Stephenie Meyer (good for unattractive teens and stay-at-home
    moms)

Classified ads

Getting the Love You Want by Harville Hendrix

Class with the Countess by Luann de Lesseps

Racing forms

*Talking with Serial Killers: The Most Evil People in the World Tell Their Own
    Stories* by Christopher Berry-Dee

Madame Bovary by Gustave Flaubert

Secrets of the Baby Whisperer by Tracy Hogg and Melinda Blau

Justin: The Unauthorized Biography by Sean Smith

Sex for Dummies by Dr. Ruth K. Westheimer

Diary of a Wimpy Kid by Jeff Kinney

Some people with whom to eat your feelings:

Stranger resting on a bench,
Stranger hiding in a trench.

Stranger sitting on a box,
Stranger winding up the clocks.

Stranger swimming in a tank,
Stranger working at a bank.

A baseball coach or Phyllis Diller,
A crossing guard, a serial killer.

Someone who is very fat,
Someone who just stole your cat.

Someone who is nice and lean,
Someone who will stop and clean (your
dishes).

Someone who is feeling cozy,
Barney Frank and Nance Pelosi.

Someone who knows all your flaws,
Jack and Jill and Santa Claus.

A friend you've known for very long,
Someone who makes egg foo yong.

The president, a Minotaur,
Mr. T, Pat Benatar.

A hot dog man, or Peter Pan,
The troll inside your garbage can.

You, yourself, and no other,
Definitely not your husband's mother.

Someone small or someone tall,
Anyone and one and all.

Some music to listen to while eating your feelings:

"I Am a Rock" by Simon and Garfunkel

"Blue" by Joni Mitchell

"Making Love Out of Nothing at All" by Air Supply

"Another Saturday Night" by Cat Stevens

"Send In the Clowns" by Melissa Manchester

"I Guess That's Why They Call It the Blues" by Elton John

"I Am . . . I Said" by Neil Diamond

"I Got a Name" by Jim Croce

"Womanizer" by Britney Spears

"You're So Vain" by Carly Simon

"Don't Look Back In Anger" by Oasis

"No Woman No Cry" by Bob Marley

"I Ain't Missin You" by John Waite

"Take This Job and Shove It" by Johnny Paycheck

"Lookin' for Love" by Johnny Lee

"Fooled Around and Fell In Love" by Elvin Bishop

"Never Surrender" by Corey Hart

"The First Cut Is the Deepest" by Cat Stevens

"Wave of Mutilation" by the Pixies

"Fifty Ways to Leave Your Lover" by Paul Simon

"Creep" by Radiohead

I'm a Loser by Doris Duke (whole album)

"Not the Girl You Think You Are" by Crowded House

"Raining Blood" by Slayer

Nothing by Michael Buble

Nothing by Josh Groban

Nothing by Celine Dion

Nothing by James Blunt

Nothing by Dan Fogelberg

Nothing by Steely Dan

Nothing by Bruce Hornsby

Some things to avoid while eating your feelings:

Conversation

Confrontation

Competitive fencing

Cage fighting

Cage diving with great white sharks

Utensils

Mirrors

Clothing

Paparazzi

Children

Skiing

Performing in the ballet

Making important speeches

Getting married

Filing taxes

Choking

Newscasting

The man

Children

Space flight (zero gravity not conducive to rapid eating)

Forensics

Scales

Video cameras

Tricky wrappers or child-proof containers

Traffic accidents (especially when eating on the go)

Acknowledgments

There are a number of people I need to thank, as this book would not have been possible without the generosity and humility of a lot of people.

First off, I am truly fortunate to have a husband who is as supportive and awesome as mine. His advice and guidance have been, and continue to be, invaluable. Thanks, Frank. To Buster and Tallulah, thank you for being patient while Mommy is immersed in the computer, and for being so hilarious and enthusiastic and imaginative and inspiring.

The rest of my family: Jason Bucha—everyone should be so lucky as to have a brilliant attorney in their family, but my brother is the best. For real. Lindsay Bernsohn and Becky Bucha helped with so many of the photos and read so many drafts and, most of all, provided inspiration for many of the recipes (not saying which ones). I love you guys. My grandmother, Mary Bucha, bestowed upon me many of the recipes herein. My mother, Carolyn Bucha, imparted still others, as well as ideas and encouragement. You used to say one day I would write a cookbook, but I bet this isn't what you had in mind. My father, Paul Bucha, and his wife, Cynthia, took part in a hilarious impromptu photo shoot at a rest stop on the New Jersey Turnpike. My mother-in-law, Josephine Timilione, has the most obscure and wonderful cookbook collection and was kind enough to lend it to me. Matt Bernsohn didn't mind me exploiting him or his employees and hooked me up with so many people to photograph. Chris Baran not only gave me photos, but drew me a super-excellent chupacabra to boot.

Many people helped me with either time, inspiration, photographic excellence, or by allowing me to take pictures of them in compromising positions, they are: Stefanie Badwey, Seth Bardelas, Nicole Brodeur, Andrew Kirk, Tuki Lucero, Kelly McCann, Marianne O'Brien, Michael Pampalone, Matthew Rudnicki, Ella Solomons, and Sophia Wood.

And finally, to my very dear friend, Luke Dempsey, who can't get rid of me as easily as he thought; the amazing Erin Malone and Jennifer Walsh at WME; Clare Ferraro, Anna Sternoff, Elizabeth Keenan, Alexandra Ramstrum, Caroline Sutton, and everyone at Hudson Street Press, thank you for making this dream come true.

Index

Index

Index

Index

Index

Index

Index

Index

Index

Index

Index

Index

Index

Index

Index